Rhinegold Study Guides

A Student's Guide to AS Performance Studies

for the **OCR** Specification

by John Pymm

with Gail Deal and Alistair Conquer

R·

Rhinegold Publishing Ltd
241 Shaftesbury Avenue
London WC2H 8TF
Telephone: 01832 270333
Fax: 01832 275560
www.rhinegold.co.uk

Rhinegold Performance Studies Study Guides
A Student's Guide to AS Performance Studies for the OCR Specification
A Student's Guide to A2 Performance Studies for the OCR Specification

Rhinegold Drama and Theatre Studies Study Guides
A Student's Guide to AS Drama and Theatre Studies for the AQA Specification
A Student's Guide to A2 Drama and Theatre Studies for the AQA Specification

A Student's Guide to AS Drama and Theatre Studies for the Edexcel Specification
A Student's Guide to A2 Drama and Theatre Studies for the Edexcel Specification

Other Rhinegold Study Guides
Students' Guides to GCSE Music for the AQA, Edexcel, OCR and WJEC Specifications
Listening Tests for Students: AQA, Edexcel and OCR GCSE Music Specifications
Students' Guides to AS and A2 Music for the AQA, Edexcel and OCR Specifications
Listening Tests for Students: AQA, Edexcel and OCR AS and A2 Music Specifications
A Student's Guide to Music Technology for the Edexcel AS and A2 Specification
Listening Tests for Students: Edexcel Music Technology AS and A2 Music Specification

Rhinegold Publishing also publishes Classical Music, Classroom Music, Early Music Today, Music Teacher, Opera Now, Piano, The Singer, British and International Music Yearbook, British Performing Arts Yearbook, Music Education Yearbook, Rhinegold Dictionary of Music in Sound.

First published 2004 in Great Britain by
Rhinegold Publishing Ltd
241 Shaftesbury Avenue
London WC2H 8TF
Telephone: 01832 270333
Fax: 01832 275560
www.rhinegold.co.uk
Reprinted 2005

You should always check the current requirements of the examination, since these may change. Copies of the OCR specification may be obtained from Oxford, Cambridge and RSA Examinations at OCR Publications, PO Box 5050, Annersley, Nottingham NG15 0DL Telephone 0870 870 6622, Fax 0870 870 6621. See also the OCR website at www.ocr.org.uk

A Student's Guide to AS Performance Studies for the OCR specification
British Library Cataloguing in Publication Data.
A catalogue record for this book is available from the British Library.

ISBN 1-904226-29-9

Printed in Great Britain by WPG Ltd

Contents

The authors

John Pymm is associate dean of the School of Sport, Performing Arts and Leisure at the University of Wolverhampton. He is responsible for undergraduate and postgraduate degrees in dance, drama, music and popular music. Prior to moving into higher education, he was performing arts coordinator at Rowley Regis Sixth Form College. He was involved with the development of the first syllabus in A-level performing arts for the University of Cambridge Local Examinations Syndicate in 1990, becoming chief examiner for that syllabus in 1994. Between 1996 and 1999 he led two development teams for the Curriculum 2000 project, the Advanced Vocational Certificate of Education in performing arts and the Advanced GCE in performance studies. He was subsequently appointed as chief examiner for Advanced GCE performance studies in 1999 and is principal examiner for performance realisation and student devised performance.

Gail Deal is a senior examiner for performance studies with OCR, an examiner for dance with AQA and an examiner for drama with IGSCE. She is head of performing arts and music at Esher College in Surrey, where she also teaches media studies and previously taught English.

Alistair Conquer has taught in Reading, Leicestershire and Nottinghamshire, and has been creating youth performance work for over 30 years. He is currently the senior service manager of curriculum enrichment for the City of Nottingham LEA and a principal examiner for OCR performance studies.

The editors

Emma Whale (project manager), Charlotte Regan (senior assistant editor), Joanna Hughes (designer), Lucien Jenkins (editor).

Acknowledgements

In the writing of a guide such as this many people have contributed. The authors and publishers are grateful to the following people for their specific advice, support and expert contributions: Hallam Bannister, Jenny Fairclough, Emma Findlow, Luke Harley, Louise Powell, Elisabeth Rhodes, Elizabeth Rogers, Bev Sokolowski and Abigail Walmsley. The authors are also conscious of having drawn on a lifetime's reading. More recently, the growth in use of the Internet has made an unparalleled amount of exciting information and challenging opinion widely available. Although every attempt has been made to acknowledge both the primary and secondary sources drawn on, it is impossible to do justice to the full range of material that has shaped the creation of this book. The authors would therefore like to apologise if anyone's work has not been properly acknowledged. They would be happy to hear from authors or publishers so that any such errors or omissions may be rectified in future editions.

Introduction

Once you've chosen to take A-level performance studies, there are probably quite a few questions that you'll want to ask. You may be puzzled by the title, for example, as you may well never have studied this subject before at school. If you've studied dance, drama, music or expressive arts at GCSE, or if you regularly take part in dance, drama or music as part of the provision in your school, college or local education authority, this could be an ideal course for you.

You don't need to have studied all three art forms before you begin the course, as long as you have developed some skills in at least one of them. So, if you've got some skills in dance, drama or music, a passion for performing, a drive to devise and perform pieces, and a mind made up to study, you should be fine.

What is performance studies?

Performance studies is a unique subject and is also fairly new at A level. It looks at the three art forms of dance, drama and music, at the way in which these work when they are brought together, and at the potential this creates for your own practical work.

Is it the same as performing arts?

Obviously, there are two key words here: 'performance' and 'studies'! You'll take part in a number of practical performances and study the way in which pieces and performances are put together. It's as simple as that – everything you do in this specification grows from one of those aspects.

There is some overlap between performance studies and performing arts, but there are also some important differences. The similarities are that the subject matter is essentially the same – dance, drama and music. The performance studies course has a lot of references to performing arts and there are probably more similarities than differences. The differences are that you will not be examined on technical or business skills in performance studies – the focus is on the arts themselves rather than their associated vocational skills.

So is it three A levels in one?

Although performance studies covers dance, drama and music, it doesn't represent three different A levels, because you don't study the subjects individually. You'll be looking at the ways in which the art forms work together, which means that you will need to develop practical and theoretical skills in all of them, but you won't cover them in the same breadth as you would if you were studying for an A level in dance, drama or music.

Glossary

Throughout this guide, we have used this icon for the first instance of a word that is defined in the Glossary section on page 138.

Web link

For numerous links on drama, dance and music, visit Rhinegold Publishing's website at www.rhinegold.co.uk.

Practical and theoretical work

You'll spend a lot of your time in performance studies doing practical work. Some of this is intended to develop your skills in communication and group work, so that you understand how to create an effective performance, and here you won't be assessed on the quality of the work you do. At other points, however, you will be assessed on how good you are as a performer.

You'll also need to be good at understanding exactly what you're doing as a performer. You'll have a lot of opportunity to think about how you can learn to perform better, and particularly about the way you might go about devising your own material as a group. This is something that those who work in the performing arts need to do all the time: it's sometimes referred to as being a **reflective practitioner**. That means you will get better at knowing how to put performances together in less time and also that you will be able to evaluate whether things are working as you go along.

Is it all about group work?

There is a lot of group work and you'll learn a lot about how to work in the performing arts by taking part in this. You'll be working in groups in the Language of Performing Arts unit, and you may well choose to perform in an ensemble for Performance Realisation. Even if you decide to work on a solo for Performance Realisation, you will benefit from the feedback of others, so don't think of it as working entirely on your own.

What previous experience do I need?

There are two types of skills you'll need to be able to succeed in AS performance studies. You'll obviously need subject skills to be able to perform in dance, drama and music, and to be able to write about what you've studied. But you'll also need key skills, which can be more difficult to learn because they are not acquired in the same way as subject skills. These include good communication skills, the use of information technology, the ability to work with others, the capacity to improve your own learning and performance, and problem solving.

When you're studying for performance studies, you'll obviously have to develop communication skills (both written and spoken) during the course, and you will probably use information technology to produce your coursework. But the real strength of this course is that you will develop ways of learning that are very different from studying subjects such as maths, English, history or science. This is because you will be working with others for the majority of the time, trying to problem-solve, exploring how to create effective performances and all the time trying to improve your own learning and performance.

Can I get into university with performance studies?

Performance studies is recognised by all universities in the United Kingdom as an approved A-level specification. However, as with all A levels, whether you can use it as an entrance qualification for a specific course depends on the course you want to study. You also need to be clear about the purpose of this subject in

Think about...

Ask yourself what experience you've had of working in groups. Does it generally go well for you or do you feel left out and unmotivated? How do you cope with disagreement in a group? Do you try to dominate? Are you a good listener? You should aim to find a balance, so that you are able to express your creative ideas in a positive way, while being sensitive to the ideas and needs of others in the group.

comparison with A levels in specific disciplines. If you want to be a music teacher or play in an orchestra, performance studies will be a very useful subject for you to study, but it won't replace music. If your ambitions are to work solely in music, you need to take A-level music as well as A-level performance studies. The same applies to dance and drama. The good news is that you are allowed to study for performance studies at the same time as A levels in dance, drama and music – so long as your school or college offers all subjects and there are no timetable clashes.

The AS course

Let's look through the three units that you'll be studying for the AS in performance studies and break down exactly what you need to do.

Unit 1: The Language of Performing Arts – written (30%)

This unit introduces you to how to work in performance studies, and most of your lessons will probably be spent doing practical work. However, you'll be **assessed on your written commentary**, in which you'll write about the skills and approaches that you've learned in the sessions.

The first thing you'll do in this unit is take part in a number of practical workshops, which should explore the elements of each art form. In these workshops you'll work through technical exercises or studies in groups, so that your tutors can be confident you have the necessary skills to be able to produce original pieces in the next part of the unit.

You'll then work in groups again to devise **four** pieces. The first three pieces each deal with a different art form and the fourth piece combines the art forms. As you work on these, you'll learn about the **performance process** of improvising – rehearsing – performing.

Each of the pieces must be about **three minutes** in length and they must be the original work of your group, rather than an existing piece by someone else. You'll also need to be clear about what the purpose of each piece is.

Bear in mind that the actual written work is what you will be assessed on. For your coursework, you'll have to produce a written commentary on the four pieces. You don't need to discuss the skills workshops, but you do have to discuss your practical work in a written commentary of between 2,000 and 3,000 words. Your work will be marked by your teachers and their marking is moderated externally by OCR to ensure that there is standardisation.

Unit 2: Contextual Studies – written (30%)

Here you will be assessed on your study of **two** pieces of work by professional choreographers, composers or playwrights in a two-hour written examination, which will be marked by examiners from the board.

The paper is in three sections and you must answer both of your questions from a different section. You will find that in each

Web link

You can find the whole specification on the exam board's website at www.ocr.org.uk. There are also quite a few other resources on the site that you may find helpful as you move through the course.

Skills workshops

Pieces

Remember what we said before about group work: you won't be able to work alone in this unit, so be prepared to learn group-working skills quickly.

Written work

section of the paper there will be a choice of two questions on the practitioner you have studied. The questions will be about the practitioner and will not make specific reference to the title of the piece you have studied. Your answer to each question should demonstrate what you have come to understand about the practitioner's style through studying their work.

In examinations from June 2005 onwards, the choice of practitioners available for study will be as follows.

Section A

 Christopher Bruce

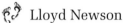 Lloyd Newson

Section B

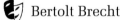 Bertolt Brecht

 John Godber

Section C

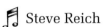 George Gershwin (at least **four** contrasting songs must be studied)

George Gershwin (at least **four** contrasting songs must be studied)

Steve Reich

You will have to memorise any quotations that you want to use in the written paper, as you will not be able to take copies of works studied or any of your notes into the examination room.

Unit 3: Performance Realisation – practical (40%)

In this unit you will take part in two performances, which will be based on the pieces you study in unit 2 – Contextual Studies. Your performances may be either solo or in a group of up to seven candidates. The length of each piece is related to how many people are performing in it: everyone must have **three minutes** of exposure during the piece. The maximum time allowed for a group of seven candidates is thus 21 minutes.

Of the two performances you take part in, one will be an extract from an actual piece you have studied. The second piece will be devised by you or your group in the style of the other practitioner you studied for Contextual Studies. Each piece will therefore be in a different art form.

Your performances will be assessed by a visiting examiner from OCR.

How to approach the course

In comparison with some other AS subjects, there may seem to be fewer books and more practical work in performance studies, certainly at the beginning of the course. This is because a lot of the knowledge you will need to acquire is gained from being involved in practical performance work rather than through academic study.

However, don't be misled by that. You still need to take extensive notes and it can be difficult to know when to do this. The essential rule is: always make notes following each practical session and keep these in a systematic format. It's probably best to keep them electronically so you can then add to them or edit them as appropriate without having to write them out again. It's likely that you will have to make handwritten notes during the sessions and then type these up afterwards.

Remember that in the coursework for the Language of Performing Arts unit, you'll have to produce a written commentary. If you have kept systematic notes of the sessions as they happen, you'll have a comprehensive record of what took place that you can develop for your final piece of work.

Preparation for practical lessons

Obviously the three art forms are not identical when it comes to the sort of requirements they have for practical work. Many of the comments that follow are most relevant to dance sessions or drama activities that involve physical work. Nevertheless, you will always perform better if you are comfortable.

If you're not sure what to wear, bring loose and comfortable clothing. Jeans are not a good idea, but tracksuit bottoms or stretchy trousers are ideal. Make sure that trousers are not dragging on the ground since you or someone else may trip over them. Avoid any clothing with zips, buckles or loose bits that could catch.

You might be asked to work barefoot and for some activities trainers might be more appropriate. Just ask your teacher for advice if you're unsure. Remember that you need to feel comfortable and at ease. You don't want to be fiddling with clothing or hair while you're trying to concentrate on a new move, or when working in a group doing lifts and support work.

Long hair should be tied up or back. Think carefully about wearing jewellery that could be dangerous for yourself or another student when doing partner work. Performance studies is not the place for a fashion statement and you may find that you will not be allowed to take part in practical work if your teacher thinks there is a danger of injury. Put a plaster over any piercings that cannot be taken out.

You will learn very early on in your course the importance of warming up before you start work. Your body is like a piece of equipment that will function best if you treat it with respect. Everyone has to develop their own routine to warm themselves up so that they are prepared to perform. Your teachers will show you how to warm up each part of the body through a series of isolations. You will need to perform and practise stretches so that it is safe to perform certain demanding movements. Your teacher will lead the warm-up and correct you if you're not performing certain exercises as instructed. This is for your own safety.

Whatever routine your teachers go through with you, make sure that you learn it off by heart and allow yourself time to complete it before each session. You must be punctual at each session. If you are late for the warm-up, you may not be allowed to take part. In particular, never try to start demanding dance work such as travelling without warming up first. It goes without saying that you

Tip

Take a working notebook to each practical session. Focus on the technical development of the work rather than just keeping a diary of who did what.

What to wear

Tip

Many examiners feel that piercings are inappropriate for performance exams. Tongue piercings, in particular, often create the wrong impression, since they affect the muscles of the tongue and therefore affect speech, often causing a pronounced lisp. Think carefully about how you present yourself.

Warming up

Tip

Notice that the noun is 'practice' whereas the verb is 'practise', so that your performance benefits from **practice**, but you **practise** your piece. If you find it hard to remember which to use, think of the noun 'advice' and the verb 'advise', which follow the same rule, but have different pronunciations and are therefore less easy to confuse.

need to be wide awake to take part in practical work so make sure you arrive feeling alert and responsive.

If you have any health problems such as asthma or injuries (current or past) you must let your teacher know before the warm-up begins. Follow your teacher's instructions and do what your body feels comfortable with. It's possible to adjust exercises for different levels of ability and ranges of movement: don't just try to do what others in the class do. Some people find it relatively easy to perform the splits while for others this is simply not achievable.

You should find that physical work only takes place in a suitable space with a **sprung** floor. Even so, some activities such as jumping require an additional awareness of safety issues. Check that the floor actually is sprung and safe to jump on, otherwise you might develop shin splints (pains going up the front of your shins). On a sprung floor that is clean and safe – make sure there are no splinters anywhere or objects that could damage you – you should be able to jump barefoot. If you are in any doubt about the safety of the floor, speak to your teacher. While trainers will help you to jump more safely, you will find it hard to 'go through the foot and point the toes' when wearing them.

You need to warm up your voice and your face for many music and drama activities and this is a more sophisticated procedure than it may sound. Many of us are very lazy with both our facial expressions and our vocal control. However, you can learn to control them both and your teachers will lead you in activities that will help your breathing, relaxation and vocal projection.

Describing practical, visual and aural elements

It can often be difficult to explain practical work in writing, particularly when you're describing movement work in dance and drama, or the notes you've played or sung in music. There are various ways in which to tackle this that are outlined below.

When you're making reference to sections of a dance or drama piece, you need to be able to convey its visual elements and you may find this easiest if you draw a diagram of the set. This will be useful for the work of the practitioners you are studying and performing, as well as for your own devised work. You can mark out where **props** are placed as well as noting where performers are in different **scenes**. Stick men are fine for this type of exercise – you do not need to be a great artist and it doesn't need to be elaborate, especially if you are in an exam. The main thing is to make it clear. If you cannot draw, then write on to your diagram where key props are situated on stage and indicate any lighting. You may also find photographs a useful tool to show tableaux and explain your devising processes.

Obviously stage spaces vary in size and form. In order to get a good idea of the size of your **performance space**, you may find it useful to pace out the stage area: pace along the front of the stage, then from the front of the stage to the back, and then across a diagonal from one corner to the diagonally opposite corner.

Web link

Schools and colleges obviously differ in the resources and facilities that they are able to provide, but even if no dance studio is available, you should at least be using flooring such as that made by Harlequin for physical work, so that your health and safety is not put at risk. Visit www.harlequinfloors.com

Set diagrams

If you've studied film, you've probably produced storyboarding, which helps you appreciate the visual image created by the piece.

See the Glossary for diagrams of different types of performance space.

When you're describing movement, try mapping it out on to the performance space. It is a good idea to think of the stage as being split up into nine different sections, named from the point of view of a performer facing out to the audience. Always mark in where the audience is positioned, since it's essential to keep in mind what they are seeing at all times.

Mapping movement

> **Tip**
>
> Always remember to name the parts of the stage from the point of view of the performer and not the audience.

upstage right	**upstage centre**	**upstage left**
centre right	**centre**	**centre left**
downstage right	**downstage centre**	**downstage left**

AUDIENCE

For marking out movements in dance, you can add **pathways** on to this diagram using different colours for each dancer. Key movements such as a turn or stag jump can be positioned on the pathways to map out the dance.

Music and sound

In your devised dance or drama work, you may be using music or sound – whether it's a pre-recorded commercial CD, an acoustic set played live, your own devised music, or some kind of live or recorded **soundscape**. Make sure you attribute this in your written commentary, making clear which track was used, who wrote it (music and **lyrics**), who performed it and so on. If it is a commercial track, then you should give details of the record label, and who engineered and produced it. Remember, though, that the more original work you produce, the better.

Musical notation

Don't worry if you can't read music when you embark upon your performance studies course. The ability to read and write music is of course very useful for composers, who need to write music that can be understood and played by performers, and for performers who need to be able to read what they are playing, but it won't be expected of you on this course. Having said this, however, if you can learn to read and write just simple **rhythms** and **melodies**, you will benefit in all the units of the course, as you will be able to be much more specific in writing about the work.

In the Contextual Studies examination, you will be rewarded if you can use short quotations from the works you have studied. If you struggle with written notation, you could use graphic notation (symbols and diagrams) but the problem with this is that there is no standard way of doing this, and the symbols you use may be misunderstood by an examiner reading your work.

The Language of Performing Arts

The performing arts are all about communication. Choreographers, composers and playwrights create pieces that are intended for performance to an audience. They want to engage the audience in order to convey their intention, whatever that may be.

The purpose of language is to enable people to communicate with each other. But think about the number of times words get misunderstood so that what one person hears is quite different from what the other intended to say. When we speak to other people we use words to say what we mean. However, there is much more to language than simply speaking words, and the way in which we use non-verbal communication is at least as important as the words we speak. We can take offence at something that is said to us simply because we didn't like the tone in which it was said, or the facial expression or **gesture** that the person made at the time. Therefore when we think about language we need to consider the way in which words, tone, expression, gesture, **posture**, **pace** and **volume** work together.

The same is true of how the performing arts communicate. There is a language of performing arts that is used when pieces of dance, drama or music are devised. It concerns the way in which the various aspects of a piece are put together in order to enable the piece to communicate to an audience.

Learning the language of performing arts

You might be worried that you have only worked in one or two art forms in the past. Perhaps you've passed a GCSE in dance, drama, music or expressive arts. You might have been a member of an orchestra, a private dance school or an amateur dramatic society. Whatever your background, there may well be an art form on this course that you haven't previously worked in.

Don't worry! This unit is all about developing the skills you already have and learning new ones. A good way of starting work is to take stock of what you already know and can do. This is called a skills audit and it will help you to be realistic about your abilities as you start the course.

You will **not** be assessed on the standard of your performance during this unit. This means that you'll have plenty of opportunities to learn skills and to make mistakes without being penalised for them. You will be assessed on the quality of your **written commentary** and we'll be looking at that on page 45.

In this unit you are required to devise and perform **four** short pieces, one in each of dance, drama and music, and a fourth piece that makes links across all three art forms. Each piece should be around **three** minutes long.

How to get good marks

Your performance skills will be assessed in the Performance Realisation unit. See pages 107–137.

Make a grid like the one below and list all the skills you have already acquired:

Skills audit

Dance	Drama	Music
For example: GCSE dance	*For example:* GCSE drama	*For example:* GCSE music
PE lessons earlier on in school	English lessons earlier on in school	Music lessons earlier on in school
Private dance lessons	Amateur drama societies	Instrumental lessons in or out of school
School productions or other shows	Youth drama groups	Orchestras/wind or brass bands/rock or pop groups
		School productions

The exam board has a list of technical terms for each of the art forms, and to do well in this unit you need to develop good technique in all of these areas. Have a look back at your skills audit. You'll probably recognise some of these words from work that you have already done.

Look up any unfamiliar words in the glossary on pages 138–144.

Technical vocabulary

Dance
➢ Motif
➢ Action
➢ Relationships
➢ Dynamics
➢ Space

Music
➢ Rhythm
➢ Melody
➢ Harmony
➢ Timbre
➢ Texture

Drama
➢ Dialogue
➢ Characterisation
➢ Physicality
➢ Proxemics
➢ Tension

Workshops

At the start of the course, your tutors will do practical workshops with you in order to help you to develop these skills. There's no point in just being able to define these words – you need to be able to apply them to your practical work and to use them when learning how to put pieces together in the three art forms. You need to know *how* to create a **motif** in dance, *how* to make up **dialogue** in drama, *how* to **compose** a melody in music. When it comes to writing your written commentary, the examiners will not be looking for definitions of words. They will want to see that you can talk about your work *using* the technical language.

You may also have the opportunity to work with visiting companies or other professional practitioners in these workshops, depending on what is available.

Your practical workshops may deal with more than one technical word. Keep notes of what you did in your workshops for reference.

Some of the words can be used in more than one art form. Look out for connections between the art forms as you go through the workshops. For example, motif appears in the dance list but is also used in music; physicality appears in the drama list but is also important to dancers and singers; and rhythm is important in each of the art forms as it links to **tempo** and pacing.

As you take part in workshops, copy out the definition from the glossary at the back of this book into your working notes so that you can compare the 'book definition' with what you actually did in your practical work.

Using skills for devising

You will probably spend a few weeks in workshops making sure you have all the necessary skills for each of the art forms. Your tutors will decide exactly how long to spend on each aspect of technique – this will depend on the balance of skills in the group.

Once the workshops are finished, you will learn about devising your own pieces. You'll have to work in groups with other students to devise four pieces. Each piece needs to be three minutes long. One piece will be dance, a second piece will be drama and a third piece will be music (these can be worked on in any order). The fourth piece has to combine all three art forms.

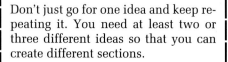

Obviously if you haven't mastered all of the skills, you won't be able to start on the pieces. You should spend extra time on your own or with other members of your group if there are particular skills that you don't find easy. Learning from your peers can be a very positive and rewarding experience.

How do I put the pieces together?

In this unit you'll learn about the performance process. This refers to the stages that you will go through in putting a piece together from beginning to end. The exam board defines this process as having three stages, although the stages are not as distinct as you might think.

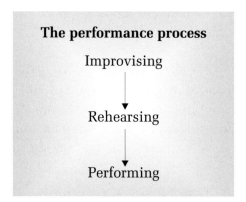

The performance process

Improvising

↓

Rehearsing

↓

Performing

Improvising

Your tutor will give you a starting point for your piece (perhaps a title, a motif or a picture). You will need to have some ideas about what you want to do with this, but don't sit around discussing it – experiment practically. Have a look at the skills you've developed in the workshops and think about how those skills could be used to create short snippets of ideas.

Improvising is all about experimenting with performance ideas. These ideas might be quite short – there are some examples on page 44. To put together a piece lasting three minutes you will need

Tip

Don't just go for one idea and keep repeating it. You need at least two or three different ideas so that you can create different sections.

minutes you will need quite a few different ideas so that your piece has some **contrast** within it. Make use of the different skills that people in your group have. Remember that you're not being assessed on the level of your skills here, so make sure that everyone devises things that they can perform well.

Once you have a few short ideas, you need to start to fit them into a **structure**. It's up to the group to decide what the structure of the piece is, but you may find it useful to agree how many sections there are before you start. Remember that each piece is only three minutes long so the individual sections will be very brief. If there are five sections of similar length, each one will only be about 35 seconds long.

Tip
Get a stopwatch so that you can time how long each section is as you work on it. You may need to increase or decrease the tempo and pacing if an individual section is not the length you want it to be.

Some types of structure that you may wish to experiment with are shown below. These are commonly used in dance and music pieces but there is no reason why they can't be adapted for drama pieces as well. You could try using a different structure for each of your four pieces so that you can compare and contrast these when you come to write about them in the commentary.

Binary form

In binary form, the piece is in two sections (both about the same length). The first half is section A, the second half is section B. Binary form is therefore sometimes abbreviated to AB.

In dance or music you could try basing a binary piece on two motifs with a brief **transition** in the middle. You could create quite an interesting effect by making the second half an exact mirror image of the first half (this is called a **palindrome**). In drama, you could have two short scenarios with a short transition between them.

Ternary form

In ternary form, the piece is in three sections but the first and third sections are more or less the same. The middle section forms a contrast to the outer sections. The first section is called section A, the middle section is called section B and the third section is called section A (because it is the same as the first section), so ternary form is often represented as ABA.

In dance you could divide the sections between the members of the group. In a group of five, two people might provide section A, with the other three providing a contrasting section B. In drama, you might create different characters for sections A and B. In music, you might write a song which has a chorus–verse–chorus structure.

Rondo form

In rondo form, the first section (A) recurs after each contrasting section, so that the structure is ABACADA and so on. In dance, section A could be slow and solemn, and the contrasting sections could be quick and upbeat; in drama try having a mimed section A, with the other sections containing speech; and in music the contrasting sections could be in different **keys** from section A.

Think of a club sandwich with the bread as section A and the different fillings as the contrasting sections.

Rehearsing

Beginning serious rehearsal on your piece means that it has now reached a state where it is finished. This is the point where the improvisation stops. It may take you some time to get the piece together but you must set aside enough time to rehearse it. In comparison with improvising, rehearsing can seem boring because it involves performing the piece over and over again to make it better.

> Allow as many rehearsal sessions as you have people in the group. For each rehearsal, one person makes comments on the performance and suggests at least one way of improving it that the others have to work on for next time.

Rehearsing is all about performance discipline. No one wants to watch or listen to a piece that looks unrehearsed, with people forgetting what they are supposed to do or even breaking down completely. You need to develop a good performance memory. You are not allowed to use written notes or music **notation** in the performance, so you must make sure that everyone knows the piece off by heart. You also need to be strict, so that no one changes what they do without the permission of the whole group. As you rehearse, you might agree that something does need to be changed because it doesn't work very well, but don't just change the piece because you find it too challenging to perform. Stick with it and rehearse the piece again!

Performing

Set the date for the performance of your piece before you start devising it and invite an audience. As the piece is only short, it could be performed at lunchtime or during a mid-morning break, but give yourself a genuine deadline for each piece as this will focus your minds and make you work more effectively as a group.

Even though the piece is very short, you need to treat it as a real performance and be disciplined in the way you deliver it. Consider the following questions:

Where will we perform the piece? As it is only a short piece you probably won't require any lighting, scene or costume changes. You could perform in the school or college hall, but a studio or a classroom might be better as this will allow you to position the audience where you want them. Think about the effect you want to create as you deliver your performance. If you have any music equipment, think carefully about how you integrate this so that the performance is tidy and, most importantly, safe.

Who should we invite? If your school or college has students doing A2 performance studies, invite them, as they will be able to give you helpful feedback in the light of what they did themselves in the first part of their course. You could also invite GCSE students in any of the art forms. It is best not to invite an audience that will intimidate you as this will make you unduly nervous. It's probably best to avoid inviting a lower-school audience as their feedback may not be as helpful as an audience of a similar age to yourselves.

Should we introduce the performance? It's a good idea to tell the audience what you're trying to do so that they will be able to give you helpful feedback about whether they think the piece worked.

How will I be assessed? You will be assessed through the written commentary you write about the work you have done in the unit. It needs to be between 2,000 and 3,000 words long (that's about five or six word-processed sides of A4 paper).

There are four assessment criteria, and you have to make sure that you cover each of these areas. We'll look at them in more detail on pages 45–46, but here they are in brief:

➤ **Knowledge and understanding of dance, drama and music** (40%). You need to be able to show that you are familiar with the technical aspects of the art forms and the way in which you used your skills to communicate to an audience in your pieces.

➤ **Understanding of links between the performing arts** (20%). You need to be able to show that you can make some links between the pieces. For example, you may identify a similar problem with all the pieces as you rehearse them.

➤ **Understanding of performance processes** (20%). You need to discuss each phase of the improvising–rehearsing–performing process and show that you understand the significance of what was happening in each phase.

➤ **Quality of language** (20%). You must show that you can express your ideas clearly and logically, and that you can use and spell all of the technical words accurately.

Although eventually you will need to be able to devise a group piece in each of the art forms, as well as an integrated piece, it is important to first think about how elements of each art form work. The best way to do this is through practical workshops. You shouldn't write about these workshops when it comes to the written commentary, since that should focus on your devising work; the point of the workshops is to get you used to exploring these elements. The activities will help you to improve your practical skills and help you to work as a group. Your tutors will have other activities to try out with you in addition to these.

Dance

You may or may not have had experience in dance when you start this course. If you haven't, this should not be a cause for concern. There will probably be a wide range of abilities in your class, from those students who've had experience in ballet, tap or modern to those who have never attended a dance class and feel rather apprehensive about the whole thing.

Some people might be put off by the idea of dance because they assume it just refers to ballet. However, while you may explore the use of ballet as a form of dance, you will be looking at a range of styles, such as street dance, ballroom, disco and **physical theatre**. Experience in any type of physical exercise will certainly help you. As long as you are prepared to have a go and not give up too easily, you will be fine.

It's unlikely that any student in the class will have tried all the dance forms that exist, so this course should be an adventure for all of you, however much experience you have. You might be able to try African or Asian dance forms and experience the fusion of

Further study

Sometimes schools and colleges organise workshops with professional companies, providing you with an opportunity to work alongside professional performers. Suggest this to your teacher if it's not something your school or college usually does.

For dance, try companies such as Union Dance or Rambert Dance Company. For music, you could find out about the percussion performers Stomp, workshops in African drumming or a samba band. A local theatre may run drama workshops, or you could look into sessions on a particular form such as commedia dell'arte.

It's also worth finding out if there are any Easter or summer workshops in your area. These often last a few days.

For the first class, your teacher will assess the skills and levels of the students and lead an appropriate warm-up. Listen to your own body and do not overwork it. The key to improving in dance is to make progress each week or each day, rather than trying to achieve everything in the first class.

western and eastern influences with dance companies such as Union Dance.

Elements of dance

You are working towards creating a dance piece lasting about three minutes that will be performed by your group. In order to prepare you for the group-devised work, you will take part in skills workshops on each of the following five elements:

➢ Motif

➢ Action

➢ Relationships

➢ Dynamics

➢ Space

Workshop 1: motif

In dance, motif is a single movement – for example the turn of a head, the stretch of an arm or the kick of a leg. A motif can be more complex than this but at this stage it's useful for you to keep things simple.

 Motifs can be put together to form a **phrase** of movement. When devising a dance piece, you can play around with the simplest of motifs to create quite intricate movement.

There are other technical terms that you'll use, such as **unison** and **canon** (see Glossary). You'll need to use these in your written commentary so it's a good idea to keep a working notebook with you – then you can jot down the new terms as they are introduced.

When improvising and rehearsing, it is useful to imagine an audience and perform to them.

Creating a motif

 Working in a pair, create a motif each and experiment with manipulating it. For example, try the following:

 ➢ Stand in **neutral**. Look straight ahead and tuck your chin in slightly. Relax the shoulders and breathe normally.

➢ Lift your right arm slowly and extend it to the imaginary audience until it is parallel with the ground. The palm should face up to the ceiling and you should feel as if you're in a position of asking for money or help. The arm should be straight but not rigid.

➢ Bring the fingertips of your right hand to your right shoulder. You have now executed the motif.

➢ Go back to neutral and perform the motif two or three times, so that you feel secure with it.

Developing the motif

You are now ready to experiment with the motif. Try the following steps with a partner and discuss the effect they might produce, on you as dancers and on an audience watching:

➢ Face each other. Dancer A performs the motif using the right arm while dancer B performs the motif using the left arm. Perform the motif at the same time and at the same speed: this is called in **unison**. As you are facing each other, you will notice that you are mirroring or reflecting each other.

➢ Stand side-by-side and look in a mirror if you have one in the studio. If not, ask another member of the class to watch you. Perform the motif in unison, with each dancer using the outer arm. You will notice that you created a **symmetrical** image.

➢ Face each other again and experiment with changing the speed of the motif. Try fast and slow speeds as well as 'stop and start' to give a more fragmented feel to the performance. Try repeating the motif three times at a fast pace and then once slowly. Discuss the effect of this.

➤ Change the **level** of the motif by kneeling instead of standing. Does the motif take on a new significance? How might an audience interpret it?

➤ Make the motif smaller and then bigger. What effect does this change in size have?

➤ Use another part of the body such as the leg to perform the motif. Take a chair and place both hands on the back of the chair. Lift the right leg to the back and keep it straight. The foot should be pointed and the toes should be touching the ground. Lift the leg slightly and then bend the leg at the knee, but not so much as to strain the hamstring. Now you have performed the first motif with another part of the body.

➤ Ask your partner to create a motif and work through the above stages.

➤ Put the motifs together.

➤ Work with the rest of the class, taking motifs from each pair, and experiment with putting them together. You could give each motif a number and ask someone to shout the numbers so that you perform the motifs in different orders to discover new and effective combinations.

➤ Consider how to make an **asymmetrical** image using a selection of the motifs.

> **Practical exercise**
>
> Having collected a number of motifs and put them into a sequence, you could now add music. Try to use 32 counts to perform the motif collection and then play some music over the top. Try different types of music: you could try a regular pop song and then contrast this with an instrumental piece. If someone in the class can play an instrument, invite them to play while you perform the collection of motifs.

Perform these short pieces to each other in the class and discuss their effects. Let a member of another small group come to direct what you do and try different devices to take the **choreography** a step further.

When your teacher gives you a stimulus for your three-minute dance piece, use it to brainstorm ideas for motifs. Poems and paintings often inspire good motifs, or a theme in a poem might lead to you creating one.

> **Think about...**
>
> If you read the words 'tightly pinched' in a poem, how could you reflect these in dance? By pinching the fingers together, pretending to pinch someone or pinching your own cheeks three times to put colour in them?

Workshop 2: action

There are five actions to consider in dance:

➤ Travelling

➤ Turning

➤ Jumping/lifting

➤ Falling

➤ Stasis (not moving).

Each of the actions should be practised and experimented with.

You will probably be asked by the teacher to move around the room. This is to familiarise yourself with the space in which you'll work. You can start off by walking and then speed up to a jog and then a run. You can change direction as the teacher instructs or change the pace. In a dance class you might be asked to skip, hop, hopscotch or walk backwards. Remember that this is all experimentation and is preparing you for your devising work.

If you are asked to perform actions moving on a diagonal across the room and you are unsure of the exercise, first watch others perform it, and then perform it with a partner so that you do not feel so nervous. Practice not only makes perfect, it also increases

> You might think that stasis isn't an action – it seems like the opposite of action because there's no motion and things remain static. However, it is a useful device because it can offer an immediate contrast and help punctuate a performance as well as create tension.

confidence, so try the exercise a few times on your own before you have to perform it in front of others.

Travelling

One of the key points about travel in a dance class is that there are other people to consider. Make sure you're aware of people around you.

 Start by walking at a normal pace in a circle so you can see everyone in the class. Choose a leader. This might be the teacher to start with. The leader should call out instructions for the class to follow, such as 'clockwise' and 'anticlockwise' to change the direction in which the circle is moving.

The circle can easily be changed into a figure of eight by creating two circles, one next to the other. Start in the middle of the room facing the audience, and walk in a clockwise circle moving away from them. As you complete this circle – you should be back at your starting point, facing the audience again – start the next circle, but this time, go anticlockwise, moving towards the audience.

Remember that the walk could be changed to a jog or a skip, or slowed right down so that you are hardly moving. Similarly, you could try walking as low to the ground as possible and then on tiptoe.

 Now work on the diagonal, often called 'across the room'. In pairs, perform triplets (which means using three steps), the first two on the balls of the feet and the third on the whole foot, as when walking. The steps are of the same duration and size. Try to stride out on the first two steps, often called 'up, up', and keep the stride the same length for the third step, often called 'down'. When executed correctly, this step allows you to cover a large area very quickly.

You should now be feeling quite warm and ready to try large hops. At first, walk by starting on the left foot and taking three steps. On the third step, hop with your right foot placed next to the inside of your left knee. Now start with the right foot so you hop on the other side. Perform these hops at a walking tempo and then speed up. Make the hop higher as you gain confidence.

 Perform this exercise with a partner, moving on a diagonal from one corner of the room to the other. Add an arm gesture and watch each other perform to develop a range of ideas. You might stretch both arms up straight above your head. You could flick the hands downwards from the wrist to add a **jazz** feel, or you could experiment with soft, curved arms for a more balletic feel.

Other ways to travel are cartwheeling, walking on your hands, rolling across the floor or perhaps being dragged by the feet. Make sure there is a space for you to perform the action and make others aware of your intentions. When you are really confident, try rolling over each other and using other dancers' bodies as a surface on which to travel.

Kicking

An action used often in martial arts is a kick, and there are various types of kicks with special names that are used for different purposes. Again, when you start experimenting, be aware of those around you. If you work in pairs, you can set up a call-and-response routine in which one dancer tries to kick the other and the other reacts, and so on. Watch each other perform a kick or two, so that you can see the ability of your partner. Some students might be able to turn and kick at the same time. You should try out the routine using shouted counts and decide on which count you're going to perform the kick. There need be no actual contact with your partner.

You can develop this action by having one dancer kick the air, seemingly at the other dancer, who grabs the first dancer's foot. From here, you could twist the first dancer's leg and they could fall to the floor using their hands as support.

 You can also use the kick in a travelling action. Start upstage right and travel on a diagonal to downstage left (see *right*). Take three steps, starting on the left foot, and on the third step kick the right leg.

The next section starts with the right leg so the left leg will kick. The kick could also be directed to the side. Perform this short routine three times in pairs. If you have sufficient space, try to perform with up to eight dancers at a time to increase the power of the action.

You or others in your class may have ideas for travelling that you've learned in ballet and jazz classes and should feel free to share and demonstrate these for others to try.

Try to put three different travelling steps together and perform them in unison with a trio, and then in canon with the whole class taking part.

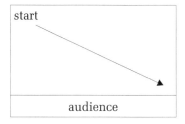

start

audience

 There are many different types of turn but let us start with a simple one.

Face front. Imagine a line parallel to the front of the stage and work along this line. Step left, then turn on the left foot anticlockwise 180 degrees and place the right foot on the floor. Now turn on the right foot (still anticlockwise) another 180 degrees and place the left foot on the floor. You have performed a 360 degree turn using both feet, and should now be facing front. Clap your hands together. Now start on the right foot, going in a clockwise direction. You should travel along the same imaginary parallel line in the opposite direction. Keep practising one turn to each side. If you turn on alternate sides you should not feel dizzy.

If you start turning and keep going with one foot leading in the same direction, you should be able to reach the other side of the room. If you feel dizzy, stop and spin the other way on the spot.

Always pick a point on the opposite wall and turn your head so that you find that same point after each turn. This also helps to stop dizziness and keeps you in a straight line so that you arrive at your intended destination.

When you have mastered the simple half turns, work on spins on one foot. You can also spin on other parts of the body. Sit on the floor, lift your knees towards your chin and clasp your hand

Turning

Practical exercise

You can use turns to make choreography more intricate. Try performing the same sequence with the dancers located on the four corners of a square and have each of them travel along a diagonal across the room. How many turns can you perform before you will collide with each other? Can you use **canon** so that dancers can reach the opposite corner without a collision?

Tip

If you want to spin fast, pull limbs inwards; if you want to stop, throw them outwards. Be careful!

Jumping

Those dancers with a ballet background could demonstrate some of the jumps they know. Jazz also has a set of jumps which are slightly freer in feel. If you have access to a copy of *West Side Story*, look at some of the jumps in the dance sequences and see how they travel. Some jumps will also include a turn.

Falling

around the front of your knees. You could try spinning on your bottom or lie flat on your stomach and roll across the floor. Watch break-dancing, ballroom dancing and ice-skating to give you ideas for turning and spinning.

 To perform this first exercise you will need to have bare feet; socks are not safe as you can easily slip.

Stand with your feet parallel. Lift your right heel off the ground very slowly and continue the lift through the foot until the toes are pointed and come just off the ground. Now reverse the movement, placing the toes and then the ball of the foot and the heel last. Perform this exercise on the left foot.

Repeat this for both feet several times, concentrating on feeling the placement of the foot.

Now stand with your feet parallel and bend your knees gently and slowly several times. When you jump, you should feel your feet leaving the floor, starting with the heel, and when you land, you should feel that you land on the ball of the foot first. You must take off and land with your knees bent.

Start with a very small jump. Think about pointing your toes in the air and try to land softly. Once you have perfected this, you can jump higher. Try four small jumps followed by two larger jumps. Remember to control your breathing – this is strenuous work.

Now stand with your feet parallel but wider apart and perform four small jumps then two large jumps.

You can also try starting with the feet turned out, like a penguin – place the feet with the heels touching and the toes in '10 o'clock' and 'two o'clock' positions. Bend the knees, keeping the body straight and the buttocks tucked under rather than stuck out. Try the small jumps and then two large jumps.

By now you will have realised that the more you bend in preparation, the higher you will jump. Large jumps take more time so allow more **beats** when putting them into a piece of choreography.

As well as jumping from two feet and landing on two feet, try experimenting with the following:

➢ Jump from two feet and land on the left foot

➢ Jump from two feet and land on the right foot

➢ Make the jumps travel in a straight line

➢ Make the jumps turn at agreed moments in the routine.

Run across the room and jump from the left foot on to the right, then try this from right to left. Do you feel more comfortable on one foot than you do on the other? If you do, don't worry – this is usual. Most dancers have a favourite side from which to start an action. You should try to practise more on the side you find less comfortable.

This demands a high level of trust – in yourself, in others and in the environment where you're rehearsing and performing. Again, use mats to help support you at first.

In pairs, have dancer A standing behind dancer B and catching them as they fall backwards. Try this several times, remaining focused. Don't stand too far away from each other.

Then try falling to the ground on your own and putting your hands out for support. You might want to practise press-ups in order to strengthen your arms in preparation for this exercise.

You'll find that letting the body relax as much as possible helps. Let your teacher lead the session and listen carefully to their instructions.

You can develop this by falling off tables and chairs – experiment and see what effects you can create. Remember that you can fall from a high and extended position into a low one without necessarily falling completely to the ground. It's a question of where you allow your body weight to take you.

Two important places for using **stasis** are the beginning and end of a performance. You might walk on stage with lights down and take up your starting position. The lights come up and you remain absolutely still until the piece begins and you are required to move. You must maintain your focus and create a strong presence on the stage. The same applies at the end of the dance piece: this is the last thing the examiner sees and you want them to be left with a positive impression. All too often, a beautiful piece of work, performed accurately and with a degree of precision and excellence, is suddenly ruined by the lack of a definite and held ending.

The dancers should count to eight at the end of the piece to allow the audience to realise that the piece has finished. The dancers should walk purposefully either off stage into the wings, looking straight ahead of them, or they should form a line and bow in unison to receive the applause before walking off. Sometimes it might be appropriate to hold the last position while the curtains close.

There are many ways to end a piece and receive applause, but any ending must be agreed upon and rehearsed until it looks professional. Don't forget that the audience will be watching you as long as there is light on the stage and you are in view.

Stasis can be used at various points throughout a piece. It might be that three dancers are moving around a fourth who is static. You can experiment with introducing stasis in unison work (where it becomes very powerful) and in **canon** for added effect.

Workshop 3: relationships

This element refers to the way in which you use dancers in different groupings, such as solo, duet, trio, quartet, quintet and sextet. If the whole group is performing on stage at once, we call this the **ensemble**. Students often think that all dancers must be performing at the same time, but you can set up a good contrast between one group on stage that has formed a **tableau** and another that is moving. This is an example of **juxtaposition**.

Stasis

> **Tip**
> Fiddling with your hair or your costume completely destroys any image you've tried to create, so remember to stay still.

One way of making a tableau is to ask one dancer to take up a wide position with their arms held out in an asymmetrical manner and the legs bent in a wide **plié**. The next dancer has to fill in one of the gaps that the first dancer's body has made; the third dancer then tries to fit in to a gap made by either of the first two and so on. The same exercise can be tried with the dancers all in a line. You could also try it using the three levels. You could also make up your own rules, such as using only one arm.

When working on your three-minute piece, divide it into sections and allow certain subgroups of dancers to make up the different sections. Watch each other to ensure continuity and check that the choreography reflects the stimulus. Try to vary the tempo of the sections to create more contrasts. Vary the number of dancers in each group – each person might try a solo. A solo can be as short or as long as you wish and you don't have to perform one if you don't feel comfortable doing so. This is a group piece and the group should decide together on the style and **form** it takes. Support work is very effective and you could try some lifts.

Workshop 4: dynamics

In dance, dynamics refers to the quality of the movement – whether it is heavy or light, gentle or rigid and so on. Some people like to think of it as the feel of the movement. Consider which emotion you wish to convey through the movement: is the movement sustained or sudden? Jerky or smooth? Weighted or gravity-defying?

Weighted movements have a heavier dynamic, with the impression that the body is drawn down towards the floor, and the limbs and torso not held up in a rigid, up-lifted manner. Movement that is gravity-defying is the opposite: typical of ballet, it makes all movement look incredibly light, almost as if the dancer is about to take off and fly. The dancer tries to elongate the body and lift the leg as high as possible into the air as if it has no weight.

Try to raise your arm to the ceiling and then touch your head. Now perform the exercise in different ways, considering each of the dynamics mentioned above. How does each performance of the movement differ? Ask someone in the class to watch you perform the move in different ways and comment on the effects created.

Those who enjoy a direct correlation with the music played as the **accompaniment** might think about the dynamic of the movement as being the way in which the dancer interprets the music. It is the way in which you perform a certain movement, and this in turn will depend on the meaning that you wish to communicate to your audience.

For example, think of a simple motif, such as lifting your hand above your head: this can be performed in many different ways. First try performing it slowly and gracefully, following the path of the hand with your eyes to make the movement elegant and suggest a high **status** to the dancer. Imagine you are of noble birth and wish to make an impact when first introduced. Then perform it by moving your hand to your head in fits and starts, with the head angled down to display embarrassment and to communicate a low status.

Further study

Various ballets on video could be recommended here, particularly the Ballets Russes, e.g. Petrushka – videos available from www.dancebooks.co.uk.

Try performing various kicks and punches into the air to experiment with powerful and strong dynamic movement, and then think about performing the movements in slow motion. What effects have you created?

Workshop 5: space

Consider the space in which you're working and how you might use it. Your teacher will probably explain the different areas of the stage to you, such as upstage right and centre stage. Some people divide a rectangular stage into nine equal parts.

See page 11 for more on how to mark out the areas of the stage in a dance piece.

 You may find it useful to mark out your dance piece on a sheet of paper and see if you've put movement into each area of the stage. Have you used some areas more than others?

Practise in the space that you're going to perform in and get used to walking on and off stage. You might have a raised stage in a school hall and thus the possibility of using the floor level as well. There might be steps up to the stage, which can also be used to good effect.

Make sure that when you are devising the piece, each member of the group takes a turn to sit in the audience and watch it. You should each give your viewpoint as an audience member. You should also take photographs of the piece as you are working on it. It's best to take photos of static positions unless you have very fast film. You could also video the piece so that you can analyse it and see where and how it could be improved.

Always think of the space in three-dimensional terms and consider the performance image you are creating for your audience.

Drama

Don't worry if you come to this course without much experience in drama, since this unit is aimed to introduce you to the basic elements. Equally, if you have completed a GCSE in drama (for example) you shouldn't assume that you have 'done' drama. While an earlier course may well have given you an insight into some of the ways of creating drama, this AS course will give you a much more in-depth knowledge and understanding.

Elements of drama

The five key terms that you are expected to become familiar with through this unit are:

➢ Dialogue

➢ Characterisation

➢ Physicality

➢ Proxemics

➢ Tension.

However, these five words are not the only vocabulary to use when discussing performance work. It's a good idea to start collecting terms as they are used in your lessons, reading and discussions.

Making notes

Scripting can take up large amounts of unproductive time, especially in class when your time available for working with others is limited. Use a production notebook, even for the shortest of performance pieces, and get into the habit of jotting down the main themes and ideas behind what is said as you devise. Let these then grow into a script when and if it is necessary.

Workshop 1: dialogue

Dialogue needs to be precise and carefully crafted. You want the audience to listen to every word, so ensure that you don't waste any. Decide what you want to get across then ask: 'How can I say it as economically as possible?' Be careful in planning your dialogue from the very start. Rather than go for the obvious, consider how it might lead the audience into feeling that they have worked something out for themselves. What do you want the shape of it to be? Which sections should be quicker in pace? Which moments require more thinking time for the character and the audience?

Remember that theatrical dialogue tends to be more artificial than everyday, spontaneous speech. The dialogue that you come up with when improvising will therefore have to be developed and adapted to make it less like your own everyday language.

Interrogatory dialogue

In particular, beware of courtroom scenes and game shows. Most court cases are long and tedious, unless constructed specifically for television, film or the stage. Game shows have become something of a banal stop-gap in devised drama when groups can't think of anything else to do. Mimicking television has to have a purpose and has to indicate a clear comment on the style itself.

Question-and-answer appears to be a simple form and is a convenient means of **exposition**, but beware – it can look and sound obvious. Decide where the questions are leading and then ensure that they are in the right order. Everyday conversations are often made up of questions and answers. Listen in to a few (discreetly!). Listen to the intonation of the voices, the sounds created by the words and the sense created by them. Listen for the ways in which the answer creates another question.

In pairs, improvise an interrogatory dialogue, with one person questioning the other on their clothing. Begin by giving fairly standard and honest answers. How interesting is this?

Then try varying the technique of how you answer:

➢ Try having no answer, or having an inability, unwillingness or refusal to respond. What might this suggest?

➢ Try a reluctant answer – brief, curt, quiet. Try this in different ways and consider the effect.

➢ Try a detailed answer giving information the audience may need.

Narration

In its simplest form, narration involves one person addressing the audience while the rest of the company act out what is being told. The next stage is to make the narration of the story interactive, with lines spoken by some of those telling the story in **dumbshow**. A step beyond this shifts the balance to dialogue between the actors, with interjections from the **narrator**.

Make one person in your group the narrator and get them to tell a simple story such as Goldilocks, while the rest of the group improvises silent actions to the story. Then try allowing characters to interject certain lines into the narration. Does this change how dramatic the scene is?

Choral speech

Choral speech can be instrumental in creating distance from the action and in stimulating the audience's response to the characters. It needs considerable practice to avoid being dull, but when it is carefully rehearsed it can be a powerful means of **narrative** delivery.

You could use a poem as a script for your group to read out as a choral speech. You'll probably be surprised at how quickly you all begin to pick up the same pauses and rhythms. You can experiment with individual voices for odd individual lines, which breaks the regularity and helps to vary the choral sound.

This is one of the most popularly exploited dialogue conventions in the theatre because it allows the audience to be part of something of which some of the characters are ignorant, which then gives rise to **dramatic irony**.

In a group of three, improvise a simple dialogue in a supermarket. Try to interject certain words or phrases that make sense in the context of the dialogue, but which, overheard and taken out of context, may well give concern to a third person who just happens to be passing with their trolley.

Silence and pause are vital tools when constructing or performing scripted dialogue. Remember that pauses can act as thinking time for the audience as well as for the character. The atmosphere created by silence can represent everything from comfortable companionship to the tense calm before the (**metaphorical**) storm. It can be extremely uncomfortable.

Silence need not mean stillness, however, since the actual spoken words are not the only means of communication.

In a group of four, construct a dialogue between two couples – four friends – over a meal. One of them has just learned that they have an advanced stage of cancer, but none of the others know. How can you make the dialogue get close to exposing that one character's situation, without making it explicit?

Now change the scene so that one other character knows. How does this change the atmosphere and the impact of the **subtext**?

Workshop 2: characterisation

When you first approach creating characters, remember that there are characters all around you who can provide inspiration. They all have characteristics that you can borrow or use as a stimulus for your own creations. Start collecting these ideas from the people you see around you.

There are many distinctions in character, but one of the most fundamental is between flat and rounded characters:

➤ **Flat** characters are two-dimensional and so have meaning but no depth.

➤ **Rounded** characters are three-dimensional and so are fleshed-out, recognisably complete human beings.

Playwrights deliberately use flat characters when they want them to represent a type – such as Mother or Soldier or a more abstract concept such as Time or Envy. It is not important for the audience to know the characters as people, but to understand the difficulties and purpose of the role they play in the drama.

Make sure that you don't all look sombre, bored and inanimate, and that your speech doesn't get reduced to a monotonous chant.

Overheard and eavesdropped dialogue

Silence and the unspoken

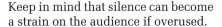

Tip
Keep in mind that silence can become a strain on the audience if overused.

Representational characters

In a group of three, improvise a scene between characters called Death, the Parent and the Joy Rider. How is the nature of the third character changed for the audience if, instead of the Joy Rider, he is called Jon or Chris?

Stereotypical characters

Bridging the divide between flat and rounded characters are those that we recognise as **stereotypes**. Stereotypical characters can be flat or round, depending on how much depth you allow them to have. The more rounded these characters are and the more the audience is allowed to learn about them, the less stereotyped they will be. Stereotypes are one of the most accessible shorthand tools available for creating character, as they rely on detailed observation that can be communicated very quickly.

A refinement of the stereotype is the stock character – such as the angry old man, familiar to us in characters such as *EastEnders'* Dirty Den, Harry Enfield's Kevin or Jim Royle from *The Royle Family*. Think of examples of the following stock characters: the damsel in distress, the sidekick, the flirtatious young woman, the naive and innocent young man – they all have their counterparts today and we can therefore exploit the tradition for our own pieces.

Hot-seating

The more you investigate how your character thinks, feels, reacts and so on, the more rounded they will become. Is your character active and in control of their world, or passive and unaware of the changes going on around them? Does the character have a weakness, a human failing, a fault?

If you studied drama at GCSE level, you are likely to be familiar with the term hot-seating. It is a devising technique in which the actor is literally put in the hot-seat, acting as the character they are playing, while the rest of the group asks them questions. This allows the performer to come up with spontaneous responses in which new insights are made explicit, and the performer can then develop these as part of the character. The technique is useful in developing rounded characters and building depth in character.

Be sensitive here. By their very nature, stereotypes can be offensive, because they attribute a set of features to a group of people, but they also provide a useful starting point for drama work precisely because they present this set of characteristics that are already grouped together and familiar.

 Each member of your group should choose a stereotype, such as Essex girl, public-school boy, American tourist, white-van driver, gossiping granny and absent-minded professor. Try to get a wide range of age, gender, social class and so on among the group. Take it in turns to be in the 'hot seat' and improvise the answers you think your character would give to questions that the rest of your group put to you.

Absorbing yourself in the role

The playing-out of a full and rounded character requires that, as far as possible, you are completely absorbed in the role. When audiences – and examiners – watch a character in performance they expect total commitment to, and conviction in, the performance.

To be convincing, every action must have a source or a reason that motivates that action, usually drawn from the actor's own experience. A psychological, **internalised** performance draws on the performer's own self to create an interior life for the character. When playing a role, continually ask yourself questions such as: 'Why is this character doing this?' 'Is it real?' 'Is it honest?' 'Does it have a ring of truth about it?'

This is a technique that you may have used already in drama lessons to develop characters. On a large sheet of paper, draw a rough outline of the character you are playing. Inside the figure, write down what you know about the character, and on the outside make notes on any assumptions and opinions you have made about them. As you rehearse, you can add new developments and new knowledge about the character.

Role-on-the-wall

Workshop 3: physicalisation

As you develop more rounded characters, you will start to consider what attitude the character will strike and how this should be reinforced throughout the piece through their physical behaviour. There is a wide range of conventional behaviours that tend to be associated with certain stock or stereotypical characters. Think of the bored teenager kicking stones along the street or the aggressive yobbo kicking in doors. What does the character's behaviour say about their attitude and what they are thinking and feeling?

Attitude and behaviour

Still working in the character roles you had in the hot-seat exercise, improvise a short scene in which your group of stereotypes are at a cocktail party. Develop your character further by exploring their behaviour. How do they relate to the others? What is your status in relation to each of the others? How will your behaviour reflect the attitude of your character?

Performance is driven as much by what you do as what you say. All too often, performers forget what their bodies can do by way of communication. Often, those new to performance feel awkward about using their body with enthusiasm and this leads to a lot of 'wooden' performances.

Practical exercise

As an exercise to start using your body to communicate, think of cartoon characters' extreme and excessive behaviour. Try creating a two-minute tale of woe presented in the style of Roadrunner or Tom and Jerry. Get in at least one run and splat into a wall, sliding down on impact. Rely on movement and gestures rather than dialogue.

The term 'physical theatre' refers to a greater awareness of the power of communication possible with the body, something that grew out of the development of dance. It is now a term we use to encourage the performer to think about the ways in which the physical nature of performance can speak for itself. Practically, physical theatre can refer to exaggerated, stylised gesture and movement, or the representation of props or sets through the body: a performer on all fours as a table, for example, or with two raised arms encircling the head imitating a hairstyle.

To match the shift towards a more psychological and emotional approach to acting, a natural use of the body in dramatic performance has also developed. In this realistic approach, it is important that the character is not just recognised or understood by the audience, but believed.

In terms of performance, our body is, literally, the tool. We can make it into almost whatever shape we wish. We can tell the audience that a character is stiff, autocratic and formal by using **body language** more quickly than we could through words. We can deliberately use body language in reactions between characters to illustrate their relationship. Just as dialogue can have an unspoken subtext, actions and gestures can communicate more to the

Body language

Tip

In order to perform in any of the art forms, you need to be fit, healthy and awake, and the importance of a warm-up cannot be emphasised enough. As a fun physicalisation warm-up, try to physically represent household items, going beyond the 'I'm a little teapot' routine to more adventurous items such as the sewing machine, the vacuum cleaner and the espresso-coffee maker!

Tip

Once you have a rehearsal script, you may find it useful to annotate it with notes and suggestions of what you will actually be doing physically.

audience than the simple activity being performed and can give away more about the character than they might intend.

In a pair, improvise a couple sitting together on a park bench. One of them is trying to be friendly, while the other is preoccupied with other thoughts and isn't interested. Don't worry about dialogue – just see what you can convey using your body about how your character feels towards the other.

Performers often worry about how to use gestures in a way that looks natural and convincing. It is true that if used merely for the sake of keeping the hands occupied, gestures can look mechanical, exaggerated or insincere; but if you are fully aware of your character, what they think and what they feel, your whole body should interpret what you are saying into appropriate body language and gestures.

During rehearsals, you can also develop the role-on-the-wall, adding a list of words that will describe the character's posture and body positions at key moments throughout the piece. But remember that this is not a paper exercise: write the words down only once you have actually struck the pose and tried it out.

Stillness

Just as silence can be crucial to dialogue, so too in performance stillness can be as important as movement and activity. A character that remains still while everyone moves and hurries about the performance space will automatically become the focus of attention. Stopping action in the middle of things can have a powerful effect, as can working a scene so that the action naturally comes to a halt.

The eyes have it

The most tell-tale aspect of a performer's physicality is the way in which the eyes are used. If you are to be convincing in your performance then your eyes must not betray any of your own feeling such as nervousness. It can be daunting to perform in front of an audience, especially if you are unaccustomed to doing so, and this is one area where you can benefit a great deal from rehearsals. Try practising a scanning technique that appears to take in all of the audience, but no one member of it in particular. Try to include your looks and eyes as part of the devising and rehearsal process in order to be using all the possible options available to you in the physical communication process.

Workshop 4: proxemics

In performance terms, proxemics concerns the arrangement of space as one of the crucial elements at our disposal. When you consider the proxemics of a piece, you are looking at the physical relationships between the performers, a given space and the audience, and how the relative positioning of these creates and manipulates meaning for the audience in a visual way.

More than anything else, being aware of proxemics will remind you that an audience is looking at your performance work. This applies to your work in music and dance as much as it does to what

The term 'proxemics' was defined as the study of our 'perception and use of space' by the American anthropologist Edward T. Hall in his book *The Silent Language* (1959). His interest was in sociological observations of how different cultures treat space between each other at different times.

you do in drama: a soloist who stands behind the piano with a music stand obscuring their head and shoulders doesn't show great concern for their audience. You should always be aware of the 'stage picture' – what the audience sees. Of necessity, and deliberately, this is constantly changing, but you must never forget that they are watching the whole thing, not just one performer – even if that performer is the intended focus, don't forget that they can still see anyone else on stage.

First, you should look at what is known as the **mise-en-scène**. You should be aware that from the very start you are constructing something to be visually stimulating as well as functional. As a basic principle, there should be a sense of balance about the picture that you make. Keep the space uncluttered, decide what is necessary and consider how it can be used throughout the piece, rather than just once or twice. Think about the significance of objects placed in the performance space: a gravestone carries much more potential impact than the predictable table and chairs.

During the rehearsal process, when someone is not involved in a sequence, put them out front to observe. Remain aware that what you are creating is theatre and not television or film: for example, a close-up shot works well on screen, but does not transfer to stage.

Having carefully established the mise-en-scène, the characters are then located, or **blocked**, in relation to it. Remember that this is an overall image that is constantly changing and therefore needs reviewing as the piece is built. The more people there are on stage, the more important this becomes.

Levels

Although often forgotten, levels are an essential tool in your kit. Consider how the use of levels communicates to the audience in each of these situations:

➤ Performer A is positioned on a raised area within a space.

➤ Performer A is positioned on a raised area while the other performers are positioned at a lower level, focusing on the raised area.

➤ The group of performers on the flat are introduced before the entry of performer A, who takes the higher level.

➤ After the group on the flat are introduced, performer A enters attended by two others, who enter slightly behind and stand behind performer A.

Each of these positionings conveys a message to the audience about the relative status of the performers on stage without any words even being spoken.

Upstaging is a deliberate proxemic convention which allows depth to be created in the relation between the characters and the audience. Upstaging often implies power over the **downstage** character(s) and almost always draws the focus. This element of proxemics can also work in reverse: moving a character downstage from a group, closer to the audience, allows them to talk to the audience directly and comment on something that has happened (an aside). It also helps to isolate the character from others.

Background/foreground

As with levels, entrances and exits are grossly underused by performers, despite the fact that they can often provide useful information for the audience and, more specifically, change the **dynamics** of a scene/space. In your improvisation and devising

Entrances and exits

In live theatre, an audience can only become fully engaged if they choose to see the stage as the world of the play rather than as a set and props. This willingness to ignore otherwise unbelievable elements is known as the 'suspension of disbelief'. However, this is unlikely to extend to believing that a particular direction simultaneously represents the kitchen, the toilet, the bedroom *and* a shopping precinct!

work, always think about how and from where the characters are going to enter.

Workshop 5: tension

Creating some sense of tension – not just between the characters, but also between the action of the drama and the audience – is the real stuff of successful scripted and devised drama. Tension can both grow from and create conflict, and it is the conflict that feeds the action.

Rubber bands

An audience's level of interest in a piece of drama can be likened to a taut rubber band. Stretched and plucked, it plays a note and can be interesting for a short while, but to keep our continuing interest we have to vary the way the rubber band is stretched and play different notes; we have to stretch it as far as it will go at some point to see if it will break. So with your devised piece, you have to create an ever-changing tension right the way through. The audience wants to watch pressure being applied and see the tension build. They want to know where the breaking point is for the character, for the scene, for the play.

With a partner, act out a 30-second scene and accompany it with a rubber band stretched between your finger and a fixed point. Trace the shape of the scene with notes on the band to indicate the points of tension.

Mapping it

You need to get a sense of where the tensions are in your script. One of the easiest methods is to create a simple graph of the scene with time on the horizontal axis and degrees of tension on the vertical axis on a large sheet of paper. Write in the dialogue or action at particular moments to remind yourself of when things change, rise or fall. In this way, when devising you will immediately see whether you have some deliberate direction and intention in the piece, as well as variety.

If you have a subplot (a secondary plot that runs alongside the main one) in a drama, you may well have two lines that intertwine throughout the play.

Climax

Climax is the term for a high point in drama. If the whole drama is maintained at either a high level of tense activity or a low level, then it will be rather tedious. You need to decide where the climax of the piece is going to be, how you get to that high point and what happens after it. There may well be mini-climaxes on the way to it, with of course the associated dip, only to rise again even higher. These dips are called anti-climaxes, but by no means imply disappointment: rather they form a necessary breathing space before the action moves again.

Stretching the moment

You need to be very careful when choosing to hold the audience's attention at a particular point; stretch it for too long and you will lose them. It then becomes twice as hard to engage with them again.

This is an easy exercise to try out with your class. In a pair, act out a version of the 'He's behind you' gag familiar from pantomime, with the rest of your class as the audience. See how long and in how many different ways you can retain that excitement and interest before the class gets bored.

You will want your audience to think about where the tension pathway in the drama is taking them, but make sure that there is always some surprise. Build the tension in a way that involves change. Sometimes you could have a sudden action that precipitates a violent rise in the level of tension. At other times, you could try letting the tension creep up on them.

In a pair, improvise a scene between two students who share a house, one quiet and tidy, the other noisy and slobbish. Try to let the tension rise between them without it being obvious to the audience. The audience should feel that something is going on but not be able to tell what it is until it bursts and they become aware of the depth of feeling all in one moment.

Without tension the drama is dead, but too much tension can also kill interest in the moment. The ever-popular soaps on television need to create a continuous stream of stressful endings to ensure that you turn on again. It is life condensed into 30-minute chunks of interesting bits. In live performance you can take a little more time to explore, build, manipulate, tease, lead and confuse your audience, because that is why they are there.

We know where you're going!

You can artificially enhance a tense moment by snapping the audience away from the action with a blackout. But this only works once: don't overdo the effect.

Music

Some students of AS performance studies become concerned because they neither play an instrument nor read music, and therefore think that they lack musical skills and thus cannot take part in 'proper' music. At the other extreme, some students have been playing an instrument from a very young age and are technically very advanced when they start the course. Although it may seem strange, the performance studies course can offer challenges in music irrespective of your background. In fact, some accomplished instrumental players have struggled because they have never been asked to consider the elements of music before! Just because you've been having instrumental lessons doesn't mean that you've ever had to devise your own material as part of a group.

Elements of music

So what are the elements of music? As with dance and drama, there are many aspects to the art form of music, and you are required to know the following five elements:

➢ Rhythm

➢ Melody

➢ Harmony

➢ Timbre

➢ Texture.

The following workshops will enable you to develop your skills to a level where you can devise an original piece of music that you can write about in your commentary.

Workshop 1: rhythm

Rhythm provides the backbone to music: imagine what a rock song would sound like if you took away the drum rhythm. In orchestral music there is not usually a drum kit, but there is generally a percussion section. Even if there is no percussion involved, the music still has rhythm. The term generally refers to the way in which sounds are grouped together in time. The effect of stringing together sounds of different lengths produces a distinctive pattern. The overall pattern can be either regular or irregular, depending on how you group them.

Establishing a pulse

It can be difficult to clap regular beats without getting faster or slower. A clock has a constant steady beat, like a heart beat. We'll refer to this as a **pulse**. In your group, clap a steady pulse. You can use a **metronome** if you want to, until you are all accustomed to clapping in time. If you use a metronome, set the speed to 72 – this is the same speed as a normal heart beat. Another word for pulse is beat. We'll use the two words to mean the same thing.

Get one person to keep a steady pulse going constantly. The rest of the group will double the speed (add an extra clap in between each pulse). When they have done that, try halving the speed (clap every other beat).

Now improvise some rhythms using these regular beats. While the pulse remains constant, each person in the group can make up a rhythm lasting for eight beats. As soon as the first person has finished, the next person in the group starts. Try to memorise the rhythm you have made up – this way you'll develop your performance memory. Keep the improvisation going until everyone in the group can remember their eight-beat rhythm.

Working with irregular rhythms

You'll quickly realise that most rhythms are not as regular as this! Most rhythms contain notes that happen in between the beats – otherwise they wouldn't be very interesting to listen to. Think of the way a drum kit works in a rock group. The bass drum often has a steady pulse (perhaps with the first note of each group of four emphasised). The snare drum, cymbals and other parts of the kit play notes that come in between the beats. If a number of the most important notes happen in between the beats, the rhythm is said to be **syncopated**.

Now improvise some irregular rhythms. As before, one person keeps a constant beat, but this time everyone else composes a syncopated rhythm lasting for eight beats. Keep your piece going until everyone has memorised their irregular rhythm.

Combining regular and irregular rhythms

In reality, most rhythms are neither completely regular nor completely irregular, but contain elements of both. So now, see if you can remember your two rhythms – one regular, one irregular – and clap them one after the other (you might need to practise individually for a few minutes to achieve this). Once you're confident that you can remember your rhythms without changing them the group can start again.

As before, someone needs to clap a steady pulse and each person claps an eight-beat rhythm (four beats regular and four beats irregular).

There are lots of ways of developing these simple ideas into a complex piece. Here are a few suggestions you can try:

➤ Change the order of the individual rhythms – if you clapped the regular rhythm first, try clapping the irregular rhythm first.

➤ Combine your rhythm with someone else's in the group.

➤ Create a palindrome from your rhythm (in other words clap in and then work out what it would sound like if you clapped the rhythm backwards).

➤ Increase or decrease the tempo of the pulse – try setting the metronome at 120 then at 50 – but keep the rhythms the same and they will become faster or slower as the tempo goes up or down.

Once you're very familiar with your rhythms, try to introduce simple movement around the group so that you are not all standing still. Experiment with members of the group standing in different places or even moving around. The proxemics of the performance will affect the way the rhythms work.

Tip

It would be very helpful if someone in the group – or one of your tutors – could notate these simple rhythms so that you can refer to them in your documentation.

Workshop 2: melody

Melody is perhaps the aspect of music that is most likely to stick in the memory. When you hear a piece of music, you may find yourself humming the tune, and that's just where we will start with devising melody – by humming a tune. Just as rhythms are built up from small units, melody is also built up from shorter phrases.

 Get one person to hum a phrase of four notes – keep all the notes the same length. The rest of the group will hum the phrase back. Repeat the process several times (about ten) until everyone in the group has memorised this phrase – as with the rhythm, this way you'll develop your performance memory. We'll call this phrase A.

Now a second person makes up a different four-note phrase. The rest of the group hums it back – just like before – and the process is repeated several times until everyone feels they have memorised it. We'll call this phrase B.

You then need to test your performance memory and see whether you can all remember the first phrase – phrase A. So the group now needs to hum phrase A. If you can't remember it, you need to go back to the start of the process, make up a new phrase A and hum it more times until you're sure you *will* remember it!

Although making up two groups of four notes probably doesn't seem like much of a melody, it has the potential to become one. It all depends on how you structure what you've got. The simplest structure is to put the two phrases together. This gives you a structure of AB – binary form. You can extend this structure by bringing the first phrase back again, although you'll need to make sure you can remember it. This gives you a structure of ABA – ternary form.

Structuring a melody

So, now you can experiment with producing simple binary form or ternary form melodies. Once you can do this, you can expand your performance memory by working in rondo form. This is where the first phrase keeps coming back, but with a new phrase next to it each time. So the overall structure is ABACADAEAFA, and so on. You can try this by having everyone in the group hum phrase A, and then go round the circle with every individual making up their individual phrase in between (these all have an individual letter: B, C, D and so forth).

Changing the rhythm of the melody

> **Tip**
>
> Just as with your rhythms, it would be very helpful if someone in the group – or one of your tutors – could write down these simple phrases so that you can refer to them in your docu-mentation.

Think back to the work you did on rhythm. Your melody at the moment probably sounds a little dull because most, or all, of the notes are of the same length. Why not go back to the exercises and experiment with short melodic phrases that contain more interesting rhythms: some regular and some irregular or syncopated.

You can then try using five-note or six-note phrases, as this will improve your performance memory. The important thing is that the whole group learns these melodies at the same time. You can also apply some of the creative techniques that you learned for rhythm to make your melodies longer and more interesting.

Workshop 3: harmony

Most music consists of more than a single melodic line. The other parts that play or sing produce a harmony to go with it. This is normally complementary to the melody and makes it sound pleasant to listen to – if so, it involves **consonant** harmony. Other harmonies may produce clashes and make the melody seem harsh or bitter. This is referred to as **dissonant** harmony.

We will start off by getting used to how **chords** are put together. Firstly, on a keyboard, play the notes C, E and G (in the middle of the keyboard) individually and then together. We will number these notes as follows: C is 1, E is 3, G is 5. This type of chord is referred to as a **triad**: it has three notes grouped in this way. There are other types of chords, but this workshop will focus on triads.

In your group, sing the note C and hold it for four beats. Then sing E and hold it for four beats. Finally, sing G and hold it for four beats. Get used to singing the three notes, one after the other, and do it from memory rather than by playing them on the piano.

Now practise splitting the group so that all three notes are sung at once. Decide who will sing note 1, who will sing note 3 and who will sing note 5. Appoint someone to count the group in and, on the count of 4, sing the three notes together to produce a chord. Hold it for eight beats and breathe gently so that you can sustain the note.

Get the group to sing the triad in C, E and G and hold it for eight beats. This triad will stay the same while each person experiments with singing a small piece of melody over it. Go around the circle, giving everybody a chance to sing their melody (probably five or six notes is enough for each phrase of melody). Your melody can have a simple rhythm or an irregular rhythm: the important thing is that it seems to fit with the chord. Experiment with this until everyone is happy with their phrase of melody.

Triads are normally consonant: in other words, they are intended to produce harmony that is soothing and relaxed rather than dissonant and harsh. Harmony based on the same chord, however, is rare, although it could be helpful if you are trying to produce music that sounds like a chant or is meant to conjure up a sense of stillness.

Changing the chord

> Now, let's change the middle note of the triad. Rather than singing the note E, let's use D. Get most of the group to sing C and G and then try singing D with it. This will produce a chord that sounds as if the notes are clashing (dissonant), and you may subsequently find it more difficult to sing. Then try singing the F rather than D. This will also sound dissonant.

We are now going to produce a simple chord sequence of four chords. Chord number 1 consists of C – E – G, chord number 2 consists of C – D – G, chord number 3 consists of C – F – G and chord number 4 consists of C – E – G. You will see that chord 1 and chord 4 are the same.

Making a simple chord sequence

> Your group is going to sing these four chords, holding each chord for eight beats. The total length of the chord sequence is therefore 32 beats. Everyone in the group will now try to improvise their own melody to fit in with these chords. Take it in turns to improvise your melody over the top of these chords. Try, if possible, to write down the melody you have improvised.

Workshop 4: timbre

We are going to move away from singing now as we experiment with different types of musical sounds. Each person's voice is slightly different, although it can be difficult to hear these differences when everyone is singing together. These differences of timbre are important because they give music character.

You can create a large range of timbres if you experiment with the different sounds available on a MIDI keyboard. Even the most basic keyboards have a good range of sounds and you need to experiment with the different timbres available to see what works well.

Identify the different groups of sounds on the keyboard you are working with. You'll find that the sounds are grouped together as families of instruments, so that all the piano sounds are grouped together, all the strings are grouped together, all the woodwind are grouped together and all the brass are grouped together. How many other families of sounds can you find on the keyboard you are using?

Instrumental timbres

> Let's start by taking the triads you produced in the last workshop. What effect does it have to play a triad using different timbres?

Experiment in your groups using different timbres to play triads. You'll notice that some timbres sustain well, others are short and need to be repeated. You could change the timbre as you change the triad. Why not try to match the mood of the triad, or any other chord, with the character of the **timbre** you have chosen? You could use a harsh timbre (such as a trumpet sound) for a dissonant triad and a mellow timbre (such as a flute sound) for a consonant chord.

Let's go back to the work we did on melody now and think about how a melody can be affected by the timbre of the instrument producing it. Experiment by composing a short melody and try to capture its **mood** by choosing an appropriate timbre.

You can then work on putting two or more of these melodies together to create a short piece. You might use binary, ternary or rondo form for this piece.

Workshop 5: texture

Finally, we shall experiment with putting different timbres together. The effect of using contrasting combinations produces different textures. If a piece of music consists of the same combination of sounds all the way through, it is less likely to hold the listener's attention over an extended period of time. In a short piece, changes of texture may be less evident than in longer pieces.

The way in which you put different timbres together involves making the same sort of decisions that composers make when they orchestrate pieces of music.

In some ways, texture is simply the result of the combination of timbres that you choose to use. We're interested in ways in which you can vary the texture.

 Here's an exercise in realising a piece that makes use of varying textures. Just follow these steps, working in your group as you did before.

➤ **Rhythm.** First of all, let's establish a rhythm for this short piece. One person should devise a short rhythm lasting eight beats that can be repeated as many times as necessary for the duration of the whole piece. If you have a large group, someone else could also **double** this part.

➤ **Chords.** Now let's use the same triads that we worked on in workshop 3. Three people need to practise to make sure that they can still remember the parts.

➤ **Melody.** Everyone else in the group is going to work out a 16-beat melody to fit over the chords. You can use ideas from before if you wish.

Structuring the piece and varying the texture

The structure of the piece is as follows. Note that the rhythm starts and continues throughout the whole piece – 128 beats in all. The letters refer to the different sections of the piece and the overall structure is ABCBDBA.

Section A	Rhythm plays for 16 beats	Rhythm then continues as chords enter for a further 16 beats
Section B	Rhythm and chords continue	One person sings or plays a 16-beat melody
Section C	Rhythm and chords continue	Second person sings or plays a 16-beat melody
Section B	Rhythm and chords continue	The first person sings or plays their 16-beat melody again

Section D	Rhythm and chords continue	Third person sings or plays a 16-beat melody
Section B	Rhythm continues. Chords stop	First person sings or plays a 16-beat melody
Section A (modified)	Rhythm and chords continue for 16 beats	

Devising your piece of music

Having gone through these workshops, you need to work as a group to compose a piece of music lasting about **three** minutes, incorporating the five elements you have worked on.

It doesn't matter in what order you approach the work: you can be creative using the techniques you've learned. Here are some suggestions for devising your piece; you can either use these as they stand or adapt them to fit.

➢ Devise a piece with the ABA structure (ternary form) in which you compose a 64-beat melody in each section and allow some spaces between the sections for chords and rhythm alone.

➢ Devise a piece based on melody. Each person in the group devises a short melody and you then decide as a group how to structure these. Give each melody a letter and use these to indicate the structure of the piece. Add chords using instrumental sounds on keyboards.

➢ Compose a song. Choose a short poem that already exists, rather than writing your own. Make sure the poem has two or three short verses and that the lines are fairly regular in length. Try to let each person make up a tune for each line, making sure that the stresses of the words coincide with the stresses in the music. Then decide as a group how to refine it so that it does not sound as if it was written by several people. Add chords that fit your melody.

➢ Create a soundscape to accompany a video clip. The extract should be three minutes long and contain several contrasts to allow you to make variations of the five musical elements.

Whichever idea you use, you need to work through the performance process of improvising–rehearsing–performing. Refine and practise the piece fully and rigorously and make sure that the final performance is well rehearsed.

You may find that you need to repeat some of the workshops to practise your skills.

The integrated piece

In many ways this is the hardest of the four pieces to produce. You will see in the specification that there is no specific vocabulary to consider for this piece and it may seem much more open than the first three. But there are some basic approaches to putting this piece together that will help you to focus your energies and produce a piece that really integrates the work you have already done.

The most important thing is that you are able to draw on the skills that you have developed in the workshops and use them to their best effect. So a good place to start would be a review of what you are now able to do in each of the art forms, and what kind of links you can make between them.

The language of performing arts

It is only at this stage that you really start to engage with the language of performing arts. Until now, you have been developing skills and understanding terms in the individual art forms. This means that you need to bring together the vocabulary that you have mastered and think about the naturally occurring links between the art forms. You will need to be clear that there are both similarities and differences between the art forms – you do not have to pretend that the art forms are all the same. Be realistic about links, and also about contrasts.

Here is a collated list of terms from the three art forms:
+ Action
+ Characterisation
+ Dialogue
+ Dynamics
+ Harmony
+ Melody
+ Motif
+ Physicality
+ Proxemics
+ Relationships
+ Rhythm
+ Space
+ Tension
+ Texture
+ Timbre.

For each of the 15 words you have studied, ask yourself the following questions and keep your response in a working diary so that you will be able to use it for your written commentary.

➢ What skill does this word refer to?

➢ How have I used this word so far?

➢ What does this word mean in dance, in drama, in music?

➢ Are there words that only seem to apply to one art form?

➢ How many of these words could apply to all three art forms?

Workshops

It is advisable before starting work on the integrated piece that you take part in some more workshops. The purpose of these workshops is different from those that you have done up to this point. In the first set of workshops you were acquiring and/or developing your skills in the **discrete** art forms. The point of this next set of workshops is to see how much integration of the art forms you can achieve.

In the following sections we shall look at some workshop activities designed to help you achieve this integration. This will help you to consolidate your skills, enabling you to devise an original integrated piece that you can write about in your commentary. In each workshop there is a commission. The purpose of the commission is to give you a focus for the content of the work. However, you do not need to worry too much about researching the commission since they are all general enough for you to use in a creative way.

The way in which you use the commission will be very important, but for the moment the purpose is to get you thinking and being creative in producing material.

Also, equally importantly, you do not need to produce finished pieces from the workshops. You have already learned about the performance process of improvising–rehearsing–performing. As you have limited time in each workshop – only a single lesson – you will only work as far as the improvising stage. This means that the purpose of the workshop is to put together the content of the piece so that you could, if you wanted to, continue to rehearse it and refine it to performance standard. This will give you some practice in deciding what sort of things work when devising integrated material.

Workshop 1: structure

You will have learned by now that structuring your ideas is a central feature of devising pieces in the performing arts. In the following workshop activity you will have one lesson to put together a piece based on a simple **theme**.

The commission

The commission for this workshop piece is *Circles and Squares*. You need to put together a three-minute piece based on this idea.

This is a fairly straightforward commission since there is no need to spend time thinking about what circles and squares are! You should start thinking about all the ways in which you can bring your creative energies together.

The overall structure

One of the most important things to get right is the overall form of the piece. One of the most common mistakes is to sit discussing the commission, come up with ideas, but then try to cram too much material into the piece. To help you know how much material you need, you should decide firstly what the overall structure will be.

To help you with this first workshop, let's assume that you have decided the overall form will be ternary. Each section will last for one minute and the whole piece will therefore last for three minutes.

You now need to decide what should be in each section, although as the third section is going to be very similar to the first section you only really need to concentrate here on 66 per cent of the piece.

Motif and characterisation

The commission has two basic shapes – circles and squares – and this should provide some contrast. We will use ideas based on circles for section A and ideas based on squares for section B.

Section A. This section takes the idea of circles. A circle is complete; it does not start or finish.

 Devise a short phrase in dance that has one or two motifs and can be cycled over and over.

 Devise a short melodic motif that might go with this.

 Devise a short statement that could be used as dialogue. You could take the phrase 'in my end is my beginning'.

You now have three ideas, one from each art form. The task is to weave these together into the first section of the piece. You may feel that you do not have much material to work with and might be tempted to try to devise some more. Resist that temptation! Instead, improvise with ways of making something much bigger out of small and simple ideas. There are lots of ways of developing these simple ideas into a complex piece. Look back at how you built up ideas in the pieces in individual art forms. The only difference now is that the content uses all three art forms rather than one. There is no difference in the approach to structuring material.

Section B. Now use the same principle to devise material for the second section. For section B, the idea is to create a contrasting section, and the idea of square shapes may help you achieve this.

Squares have four sides and can fit together in a way that circles may not.

 Devise a short phrase in dance that has four short motifs to represent the sides of the square.

 Devise a short melodic motif that might go with this, perhaps based on four long notes or four sets of notes. You could sing the numbers 1 2 3 4 using three-part harmony (as in Philip Glass' opera *Einstein on the Beach*).

 Devise a contrasting short statement that could be used as dialogue. You could take the phrase 'on every side there is a corner'.

Section A (repeated). This is likely to be very similar to the opening section, although you may want to make some minor changes so that it is not totally predictable. The reason for having a section so similar to the opening is to create a sense of wholeness and completeness for an audience. Memory is an important aspect of performance, both for performers and for audiences. Pieces that never repeat anything can become tedious since there are no reference points for the audience to look out for.

Workshop 2: space and movement

All performance must move forward. A piece that does not go anywhere is likely to be difficult for an audience to appreciate. However, there are different ways of doing this. In western art forms there is frequently a sense of linear progression. The most obvious example of this is the way in which we tell stories. Fairy tales start with 'once upon a time' and end with 'lived happily ever after'. The progression of the story from start to end is therefore predictable.

For the purpose of devising these pieces you do not need to worry about linear progression. Many candidates for AS performance studies want to tell a story. The problem with this is that you are likely to want to spell out all of the details rather than allowing things to stand on their own. In this workshop you will use some ideas from drama together with music and dance but you will not tell a story.

In this workshop you will devise the first half of a piece in binary form (AB). This will last about 90 seconds.

Everyone in your group has a letter V, W, X, Y, Z etc. They are going to make up a sentence of no less than ten words that sums up their present state of mind. Examples might include:

V　I am not interested in watching the news as it bores me

W　I have been badly hurt and I cannot trust anyone now

X　I live to work and my money is my security

Y　My family does not understand what I am going through

Z　I am under pressure to give in but I must be strong.

This is the whole of the dialogue in the piece. You will now create characterisation through the way you use these lines. Improvise with different ways of speaking these lines. Once you have done this, try singing your phrase rather than speaking it. The melody does not have to be elaborate but it needs to have shape and use the same rhythm as the words. This style of singing is known as **recitative** and is used extensively in some types of opera to move the story along.

Now begin to use the space more so that the proxemics of the performance are an important factor. Whether you decide to speak or sing the phrases, they will seem very different depending on which part of the space you use and how close or distant you are to the other members of the group. You could start by being in a circle, and then expand the circle until you are in different parts of the performance space.

You could also use different levels to show the status of the person speaking; you could use different levels of intensity of volume. You could use different tempos so that some people deliver their phrase quickly, others steadily. All of the phrases do not need to happen at once.

Now start to physicalise the use of the phrases. Think about the quality of movement that best reflects what the character is saying. Movements could be elegant or graceful, exaggerated or grotesque, depending on the nature of the character you are trying to create. Once you have decided on the movement content, review the style of the recitative (if you chose to use it) and consider whether it matches the style of the character you are trying to create.

Once you have done this, structure the 90 seconds of material for the section that you need so that you would quickly establish these characters in the minds of your audience if the piece were to be performed.

Workshop 3: tempo, pacing, dynamics, intensity

Apart from structure, the next most important feature of effective performance is the speed at which the piece moves along. This is referred to as the pacing of the piece, and the golden rule is that you must try to achieve contrast.

A piece that moves along very slowly is likely to become dull and the audience will lose interest. On the other hand, a piece that moves along at a breakneck pace will probably be difficult to follow as things are happening so quickly. This could prove frustrating for the audience as they struggle to keep up.

In good performance, there are sections that move quickly and others that move steadily. While some pieces of music maintain the same tempo throughout, the purpose of this workshop is to help you think about ways of making your performance look and sound interesting through effective contrasts.

Look again at the piece you have just devised in workshop 2. How many contrasts are there in it? Try to estimate the pulse of the piece – the speed at which things move along. To help you with this, use a metronome. Set the metronome to 72. Does that seem faster or slower than the action you have created?

How could you vary this? Try introducing changes of tempo so that you have 30 seconds of rapid movement, 30 seconds of slower pacing and then return to the first tempo for the final 30 seconds.

Now try introducing changes of dynamics (in sound and movement). What effect does this have?

Devising your integrated piece

Having gone through these workshops you should now work as a group to devise your integrated piece, lasting about **three** minutes.

Start with a commission

You may choose – or your tutors may give you – a commission to base your piece on. This will save you a lot of time in getting your ideas together.

Here are some commissions you could use:

➢ *I danced in the morning when the world was begun*

➢ *The colour yellow*

➢ *It don't mean a thing if it ain't got that swing*

➢ *Send in the clones*

➢ *Palindrome.*

There is no need to spend a lot of time discussing the commission. Instead, experiment practically with it, just as you did in the workshops.

Agree on the structure

Your group needs to decide on the structure of the piece. Whether you decide to use a standard structure such as ternary or rondo or just to identify the sections you intend to use, write it down and stick to what you are trying to do. Even if you change this during your working process, it is still better to have a clear plan.

Make links before you start

There is a very important rule here – do **not** start with drama and then try to slot the other art forms in, since you will almost certainly end up writing a mini-musical or a soap opera with some music and some movement. Keep the content simple (as in the workshops) and then allow the art forms to develop naturally rather than as part of a story. You may have noticed that none of the suggested commissions above has a 'story' to it. This is deliberate – we want you to avoid telling a story.

Use contrasts

You need to use the three minutes wisely. Once you have the piece broadly structured and created, you need to spend some time rehearsing it. You will find that it is easier to spot the need for contrasts once you start to rehearse. Get the stopwatch and metronome and take it in turns in your group to act as 'director'. If the piece is too long, rather than simply cutting a section, make suggestions as to how it could be sped up.

Written commentary

The assessment of this unit is based on the written commentary in which you will write about the work you have done in this unit. You will have been working in your groups to develop your practical skills and will have devised your four pieces, and there will probably be at least some parts of these pieces that you would like to be assessed on. All we can say is be patient – 40 per cent of the whole AS is based on practical assessment, but this is at a later stage when you've had the opportunity to develop your skills further.

So what's the best way to go about producing the written commentary? It needs to be between 2,000 and 3,000 words long (about five or six word-processed sides of A4 paper). This may seem quite long in comparison with the length of the coursework you did for GCSE, so it is probably best to break this down into more manageable sections.

Let's be clear first of all about what you are trying to achieve in your written commentary. You need to be sure that you focus what you write so that it matches what the examiners are looking for. There are four assessment criteria for the written commentary: knowledge and understanding of dance, drama and music; understanding of links between the performing arts; understanding of performance processes; and quality of language.

Knowledge and understanding

Your written commentary needs to discuss examples of the practical work that you have completed. Don't spend time discussing the skills workshops that you did at the start of the unit; rather, try to focus on examples from your pieces to show that you understand the importance of skills and techniques in the three art forms and how you used these in your pieces.

Understanding links

Now that you have finished your four pieces, look back at them and see what links you can find between the art forms. You might be tempted to rely on your fourth piece alone to discuss links, as this piece is the one where you are required to link the art forms. It is important, though, for you to reflect on all four pieces and make some connections retrospectively. For example, you might feel that the pace of each of the pieces was too slow and that you had to work hard as a group to keep the piece moving. Or you might decide that structure was easier to create in dance and music than it was in drama.

> **Tip**
> Compare what you did in all four pieces and make a list of similarities and differences between them.

Think about the technical language you've learned and try to make some links. You could give some examples of how rhythm, tempo, pacing, contrast and so on applied to all of your pieces. Maybe physicality was an important factor in each of your pieces. Perhaps your drama work seemed like you were just delivering the lines rather than acting them out. Maybe your dance work was too static or your singing did not involve enough expression.

Most importantly, when talking about links, the examiners do **not** want you to try to force links where they do not exist. It is clear that there are some links that you can see fairly easily. For example, you might have devised motifs in your dance piece and you might have composed motifs in your music piece. There may be something

> **Tip**
> Studying performance studies is about seeing what dance, drama and music have in common, as well as acknowledging that each art form has many elements that are unique to itself. Be prepared to recognise what is similar and what is different.

about the motifs themselves – or the way that you used them – that is similar in both pieces. On the other hand, it may be that your drama piece had a narrative structure but this was not true of the dance or the music piece. Acknowledge these differences – this is all part of the written commentary.

Performance processes

In your commentary, you need to discuss each phase of the improvising–rehearsing–performing process and show that you understand the significance of what happened in each phase. Use this three-part structure to organise your written commentary. That way you can make sure that you don't forget anything and that you have plenty of examples for each aspect of the devising. We'll spend more time discussing the structure of the commentary later on. It's probably best to group together all your examples under each heading. You might start to make notes to gather your thoughts together.

Here is how your plan might look for the improvising section:

Plan of section on improvising
- Explain that intention of each piece was different but were some things in common: summarise purpose of each piece.
- Were given set form for each piece: ABA (ternary form).
- Started with motif in dance and tried to extend this. Examples of motif: maybe notation or a picture?
- Music: piece began with short melody: give quotation of melody.
- Drama: piece began with developing characterisation – old man gives short monologue.
- How moved on from here: discuss how improvised around these basic ideas.
- Give examples of how contrasting middle section was created.
- Discuss how first idea brought back in the final section.
- Integration: talk about how fourth piece integrated art forms – made some links by using same structure for each piece, but in integrated piece used dance and music in first and third section, and drama and dance in middle section. Give examples of why we did this.
- Evaluate: process not straightforward. Spent long time devising character in drama piece – meant pacing was too slow. Didn't spend long enough developing dance motif – meant piece was very short. In music, melody was short but helped us create another melody in integrated piece.

Quality of language

You must demonstrate that you can express your ideas clearly and logically and that you can spell all of the technical words accurately. However, this is not just a spelling test – it is important that the style and tone of what you say is appropriate as well as spelling technical words and any names of practitioners properly.

Have a look at the following three examples of writing. They should give you a good idea of what is **not** appropriate!

We loved the workshop that Pippa taught us. It was really exciting to take part in a dance workshop as I have never studied dance before and I really lacked confidence. But Pippa brought out the best in all of us. Except Sarah who was frightened and found it difficult to balance properly. In our piece we had the title 'Indifferences' and Sarah fell over...

This first example simply tells the story and reads like a diary. Most of the information is narrative and the examiner would not have any idea of why you were doing the activities.

> The rythum of our music piece was very big and we worked on adding lots of texture so that it helped the proxemics we added to our dance. Proxemics was alot better after we worked on the texture to engage the audience and they liked it and said that it was very compelling.

The second example has some spelling errors and seems just to throw in technical words without giving any indication of understanding them.

> Motif in dance is where you put together some movements to make a dance. You can use the human body in lots of different ways to make a motif. In music we made up a rhythm. Rhythm is where you do not have any tune but you might play it on a tambourine. In drama, we invented characters. This means they all had a personality that the audience could see.

This third example would get a little credit but it spends most of the time giving definitions of what the words in the specification mean. You can assume that the examiners will know and understand the technical words that you have been learning so make sure that you don't waste time giving them definitions. Instead, use technical language to discuss the pieces.

Also avoid giving anecdotal comments about matters that are not relevant – you may think that it's nice to set the scene by mentioning the weather or why one of the members of your group was late, but it's not what you have been asked to do! Equally, avoid discussing the work of other practitioners that you have observed. Keep in mind always that you are writing about your own performance work.

This fourth extract is a much better example of what you should be aiming at in your written commentary.

> We decided to begin our work on characterisation by improvising a number of stereotypes. We thought it would be easiest to begin devising with stereotypical characters because it would give us certain assumptions on which to build and which we could use in our interactions with the other characters in the group. If we had just started off with names or occupations, for example, we would not have had so many ideas of what the attitudes and behaviour of these characters would be. We all improvised dialogue with one another and this helped us to develop our roles into more rounded characters because we were made to think about their reactions to other types of character. I had taken the role of a prim and proper librarian, while Rob was playing a reckless thug, so we immediately had a clash of attitudes that we could improvise dialogue on.

Collecting information

You'll see from the previous section that we are recommending that you structure your written commentary in a particular way. Although you could simply write a short section on each of the

Tip
Remember to make clear what your starting point was when writing your commentary. If, for example, you began with a photograph, then you should give the title of the photograph and the name of the photographer, and, if possible, scan the photograph into your commentary so that the moderator will be able to see it clearly.

Structure

practical pieces, you may risk duplicating what you are saying. Try structuring your commentary so that you have an introduction, a conclusion, and three main sections. For example:

The introduction and the conclusion only need to be fairly short – about 150 words each. That will allow you between 700 and 900 words on each of the main sections. We have already suggested that you list all of the examples from the four pieces under each of the headings. You may find it useful to answer these questions as you work through the commentary. There are many questions you could answer and your tutors will probably think of others that will suit the work you have done. Try answering these and you may find that if you can use plenty of examples from your practical work, the commentary will begin to take shape very quickly. Feel free to make up your own questions as well.

Introduction
➢ Write three sentences about each of your four pieces to make it clear what you were trying to achieve in each one.
➢ Give examples of any links between the art forms that you expected when you began work on this unit.

Improvising
➢ How did you start to create your dance piece?
➢ Did this have any similarities to the drama or music piece? If so, what were they? If there were major differences and the material seemed not to have much in common, why was this?
➢ What was the **structure** of the four pieces? Did they have anything in common?
➢ Were there any problems in agreeing on the shaping of the pieces?
➢ Give relevant examples of how you used the elements of motif, action, relationships, dynamics and space in your dance piece. Were any aspects more important than others? If so, why was this?
➢ Give relevant examples of how you used the elements of dialogue, characterisation, physicality, proxemics and tension in your drama piece. Were any aspects more important than others? If so, why was this?
➢ Give relevant examples of how you used the elements of rhythm, melody, harmony, timbre and texture in your music piece. Were any aspects more important than others? If so, why was this?

➢ Are there any photographs of your work that would help to show how it took shape? For each image, add at least 50 words to describe what it shows and why.

➢ Are there any quotations from books or other sources that your teacher has given you or that you have found yourself that would be helpful? If you include quotations, make sure you add 50 words of your own to say why each quotation is important to your work.

➢ Are there any extracts from notation or diagrams in dance or music to help the reader understand what you were trying to achieve? Only include these if you intend to discuss them – there's no point in including them just to make the page look nice.

Rehearsing

➢ How long did it take before you felt that the four pieces were at a stage where you could begin to rehearse them seriously?

➢ Did you have to make any changes to any of the pieces as you rehearsed them?

➢ What were the main challenges in rehearsals?

➢ Give one example from each piece of something that you had difficulty with and had to work on in rehearsal.

➢ Give examples of something that was useful in more than one piece. For example, did you use the space in the same way, work on the pacing, adapt the piece in the light of feedback from your teacher?

Performing

➢ When did you perform the four pieces?

➢ Who was in the audience for each piece?

➢ Why did you want to perform the pieces to these audiences?

➢ What information did you give to the audience before you performed each piece?

➢ What reaction or feedback did you get from the audiences?

➢ What physical preparation/warm-up did you do before you performed?

➢ Did your pieces achieve what you set out to achieve?

➢ Did you create the effects that you intended to?

➢ Did you achieve the audience reaction that you expected?

Conclusion

➢ Write a paragraph about what you have achieved through devising the four pieces.

➢ What general points have you learned about the process of improvising–rehearsing–performing that you will be able to use in future pieces of work?

Contextual Studies

Tip

While it is important that you know about the social and historical context of the practitioner because this will aid your own understanding of their work, make sure that you do not get bogged down in the exam with irrelevant biographical material. Write about the pieces you've studied and make reference, where appropriate, to the practitioner's life – but you can assume that the examiner is already familiar with the details, so don't waste time on long explanations.

Exam board

There are three sections on the written paper and the only rule is that your two practitioners must occur in different sections of the paper. Remember that even if you study a practitioner from each section, you must only answer two questions. If you answer more than two, only two will be marked.

In this unit you will be assessed on how well you understand the way in which performing arts pieces are put together, and the way this indicates the overall style of a particular practitioner in dance, drama or music. You will also need to understand the historical and cultural context in which these pieces were written. You will be examined on two different pieces, though your teachers may teach you three pieces to give you more choice of questions in the two-hour written examination.

The pieces that you study in this unit will also form the basis for your practical work in the third unit, Performance Realisation. You will get the chance to perform the pieces you are studying or devise your own piece in the same style. This is because the examiners think you learn best in the performing arts when you do so through practical work. But always remember that your practical work will be assessed separately from your work in Contextual Studies. In this chapter, we will be focusing on the 'studies' aspect of performance studies. Later, in Performance Realisation, the focus will be on performance, as we shall be focusing on your abilities as a performer. You need to develop your intellectual skills as well as your practical skills – the marks for the two units are separate. You might be an excellent performer but struggle with understanding how the pieces are put together. On the other hand, you might be a reluctant performer but really enjoy analysing pieces of dance, drama and music.

What do I have to study?

As we've already said, you will have to study the work of **two** practitioners. It is common to speak of a dance practitioner, a drama practitioner or a music practitioner. It is less common to speak of a performing arts practitioner, because the art forms in western culture have often developed separately from each other. However, this will undoubtedly change over the course of the 21st century, as practitioners in the art forms work more closely with each other.

A practitioner may be someone who **devises** pieces for performance, or someone who performs work (their own or that of others). The practitioners available for study at AS level are all people who have devised their own work. In some cases they are performers as well but the reasons you are studying them are:

➤ They have devised pieces that are considered to be excellent examples of dance, drama or music in themselves

➤ They represent important trends in 20th-century and early 21st-century approaches to performing arts

➤ Many of their works will be performable by you.

Who are the practitioners?

The practitioners set on the written paper from June 2005 onwards are listed below:

 Christopher Bruce

 Lloyd Newson

 Bertolt Brecht

 John Godber

 George Gershwin (at least four contrasting songs)

 Steve Reich.

Later on in this chapter, there will be actual examples of pieces you could study for each practitioner. No matter which two practitioners your teachers choose for you, you must study one piece (though for Gershwin a set of songs counts as a single piece).

The choice of piece is important because it needs to show you a lot about the work of that practitioner. As a result of devising previous pieces, each one will have developed a particular style, a way of doing things that is unique. When you study a piece by a practitioner on the list, you need to know what it is in the work you've studied that reveals his style. What does he do that lets you realise it's his work rather than someone else's? We will refer to these elements as the practitioner's 'fingerprints'. Each of the practitioners on the list has his own fingerprints. You need to know what each practitioner does that is unique to him and which things are more general.

> Discuss with your teachers why they chose the piece you are studying. Why is it a good example of this practitioner's style? Why did they choose this one rather than another one you have heard of?

Although you'll only be studying one piece by each practitioner, you'll need to know how these fingerprints can be seen in other pieces that he has devised. Always be on the lookout to make links between examples from other pieces. Your teachers will give you some examples of fingerprints from other pieces to help you see how a practitioner's style develops from one piece to another.

What do I need to know for the exam?

One crucial aspect of the examination is that you have to remember the pieces well so that you can discuss them in detail. You may find that in some of your other subjects you are allowed to take copies of a work into the examination with you. However, you will **not** be allowed to do this in performance studies because it is difficult to be consistent across the art forms – play texts are far more accessible to everyone than dance notation and often musical notation. Besides, the examiners want you to develop performance memory as a way of remembering the pieces you've studied.

Tip

There's no easy way of learning examination technique! One way is to practise on questions from previous sessions. Ask your teachers to give you practice questions to work on and make sure you try to answer them in the same time that you will have in the exam – one hour per question.

On the subject of consistency, you may find that the pieces you study are of quite different lengths. A play by Bertolt Brecht, for example, might take two hours or so to perform whereas four songs by George Gershwin might only last about 12 minutes. How can this be fair? The answer is that the skills involved in analysing a short piece are more intricate than in analysing a long work. In the case of a song, you need to engage in very detailed analysis; in the case of a whole play you will be more selective in looking for examples of trends in the play. The upshot of this is that you will be expected to deal with each work in a similar manner regardless of length.

Obviously, you will not be expected to learn an entire play off by heart; instead, you need to make a list of useful and important quotations that you can use to back up the points you are making. You won't know in advance exactly what the questions will be asking you, but if you have suitable quotations for the fingerprints of your practitioner, then you should be able to apply these in your exam answer.

Tip

Don't expect the questions to be about only one of these aspects – it's common for a single question to ask you about more than one aspect.

While we can't tell you the actual wording of the questions that will be set in the exam, we can give you some strong clues as to the sort of questions that are likely to come up. There are four aspects of each of the pieces you study that you need to be completely familiar with.

Structure and form

All pieces of dance, drama or music have a structure. You will have learned from your work in the Language of Performing Arts unit that understanding structure is a vital component in understanding a work of art. Once you have had some experience of devising your own material, you quickly realise that an importance principle is not how much material you have, but how well you organise it. In an effective piece, some ideas or motifs will come back time and time again. Other ideas will only occur once – these may be used to move the piece on or create contrast and surprise. You need to know how your practitioner organises his materials within the work you are studying, and the various effects this organisation produces.

Making a map

The most important thing when you first start to look at the piece is that you get a good idea of what it is like as a whole before you start breaking it down into individual sections. Regardless of which piece you're studying, you need to have a sense of the big picture. You also need to be completely familiar with the order in which things happen. The best way to do this is to 'map' the structure on to a single piece of A4 paper.

Work through the making of the map with your group, as each person will have noticed different things about the piece. When the map is complete, review it and agree with your teacher which aspects are most important and which are less significant.

Section length

Agreeing where the sections start and end can be awkward in some pieces, and will often depend on the format in which you are studying the piece. In dance, it is likely that you will be working from video or DVD recordings, although you may also have notation available to support your study. The dance works of Christopher Bruce and Lloyd Newson and DV8 are available on video. These may be regarded as definitive performances, as they have the endorsement of the practitioners themselves. You need to be able to discuss the movement content in relation to the theme or narrative of the piece. In particular, you need to be able to show to the examiners that you understand how the practitioner uses the elements of dance to communicate his intentions to the audience. In the case of Christopher Bruce, you might discuss the use of tap dance within *Swansong*. In the case of Lloyd Newson, you could look for moments that call for great physical risk on the part of the performers.

If you're studying a play, it will normally be obvious where the various scenes start and end from the playwright's directions. However, some scenes will be longer or shorter than others and the long scenes may be composed of two or more shorter sections. You need to do more than simply list what happens, however. The structure of a play is much more than the sum of what occurs in the individual scenes. You may find it helpful to produce a structure wheel or grid to list what happens in the plot. If you're studying a play you will probably have the text in front of you as you study. Since drama relies on dialogue in a way that dance and music do not, the printed text is a standard means of preserving a play for future performances.

Tip

To create a structure wheel, draw a circle on a large sheet of paper. Divide the circle up into segments, akin to the spokes of a wheel. In each segment, note down the details of a section. As you explore the piece in more depth, you can use different shades of colour to represent the changing mood or tone of the piece.

Music may be studied from either a **score** or a recording. To be able to appreciate the structure of the piece, it is helpful if you are able to follow it from the score, as this will give you a visual impression of where you are in the piece. When you make your map, try to learn the most important motifs using music notation. This will make it much easier for you to talk about the piece in the written exam. If you're studying a song by George Gershwin, you need to be able to quote from the melody, refer to the rhythm and show that you understand the harmonies. In a piece by Steve Reich, the individual elements may consist of short repeated motifs, speech samples or rhythmic ideas. You need to be able to quote examples of these and to show you know where they occur.

Look carefully at the transitions in the piece. When it comes to devising your own piece, transitions are really important; in professional work they often occur so effortlessly that you may not even notice them.

See page 11 in the Introduction for more advice on how to illustrate movements or positions in dance.

Now that you have a map of the piece as a whole, look out for any ideas, themes or motifs that occur more than once, either in the same section or in different sections. These are structural elements that the practitioner uses to establish ideas in the minds of the audience. Make a list of the ideas that recur in the piece and compare these with the list of fingerprints for that practitioner later on in this chapter.

Elements of the performing arts

This refers to the way the practitioner exploits the elements of the performing arts. While the performance vocabulary you learned in the Language of Performing Arts unit is not exhaustive, it does give you a good idea of the fundamental elements, which in turn will give you a solid foundation for the study of pieces in this unit.

What you need to understand is how the practitioners you are studying use these elements in order to create specific works. Each practitioner has a different way of using them, and the combination of individual elements produces a distinctive style.

Further study

Look again at the performance vocabulary you learned in the Language of Performing Arts unit. What additional vocabulary will you need in order to cover the elements of performing arts used in the works you are studying in this unit? The glossary on pages 138–144 of this guide may give you some ideas.

When the exam board talks about style, it means the particular arrangement of these elements created by the practitioner, and the effect that this combination has in performance. In particular, you need to consider the effect that the practitioner wants to have on the audience.

Much of the work by the specified practitioners will allow you to see how elements of other art forms can also be integrated into the performance of the piece. Be aware of the potential links, for example, between drama and music in the work of Gershwin, between dance and drama in the work of Lloyd Newson and DV8 or between music and drama in the plays of Bertolt Brecht. Don't force this, though – the practitioners intended to produce pieces within their own art form, after all.

Stylistic influences

Despite what we said earlier about practitioners having fingerprints, no one's style develops in complete isolation. Once you have identified the individual stylistic elements of the pieces you have studied, you next need to make sense of the style the practitioners are working within. Is there an overall term for this style? For example, in the case of Brecht, you might use the term
 epic theatre to describe Brecht's intentions for the piece. The term **physical theatre** might be used to describe the work of Lloyd
 Newson; **minimalism** might be used to describe Steve Reich's early compositions.

However, you need to know a lot more than just the name of the style that your practitioner is working in. It is very important that you have an understanding of what that style is all about. You need to ask the following questions:

➤ Which style label best describes the work of the practitioner I'm studying?

➤ What other practitioners have worked or are working within this style?

➤ Which particular pieces by other practitioners are clearly in the same broad style as the piece I'm studying?

You will get credit in the written examination if you can show you understand how the piece you have studied is similar to and different from other works in the same style.

Make a list of other works in the same style. Include one other work by the practitioner you are studying and three other works by different practitioners. For each piece that you mention, list as many examples of how that piece uses the same style as you can.

Cultural, historical and social context

In order to make sense of the pieces you're studying, you need to know how they fit into the practitioner's style, but you also need to know how this style itself fits into its cultural, social and historical context.

For this you need to explore the extent to which the practitioner's place in history, culture and society has influenced his approach to the creation, selection and organisation of his material. This can sometimes be quite complex. You need to demonstrate clear links between specific aspects of the piece that you are studying and what was going on at the time the piece was written.

For example, if you are studying Christopher Bruce's *Swansong*, you will probably have come across the term 'eclectic', which is used to describe work that brings together a number of quite different stylistic elements to create a new style. However, if you take this a stage further, you can see that this a good example of postmodernism, an approach that seeks to use elements of earlier styles in a way that does not make value judgements about whether some are better than others. Ballet, for example, can exist alongside tap dance in Bruce's work. This approach has been increasingly popular since the 1960s and you will have an opportunity to study this **genre** in more detail in your A2 studies.

If you are studying Bertolt Brecht's *Mother Courage*, you will be aware that the play is often referred to as being in the style of epic theatre – but a more general description might be political theatre, since the play seeks not only to entertain its audience but also to make them think and reconsider their attitudes to the world around them. Political theatre aims to reshape an audience's understanding of contemporary events. This type of theatre is not restricted simply to the work of Brecht – indeed, many classical Greek plays could also be described as 'political' – but for this course you need to focus on the context of political performance in the 20th century.

If you are studying the songs of George Gershwin, you will need to know about the way in which popular American songs developed in the early part of the 20th century. You do not need to be able to write extensively about Tin Pan Alley (for example), but you do need to be able to discuss how the songs of Gershwin take the fairly simplistic formulae used by those songwriters and transform them into works of considerably greater length and complexity.

Christopher Bruce

Born in 1945, Christopher Bruce suffered damage to his legs from polio and his father introduced him to dancing when he was 11, hoping that it would help strengthen them. Bruce attended the Benson Stage Academy in Scarborough and was trained in ballet, tap and acrobatic dancing. At the age of 13, he went to the Rambert School and at 18 he joined Ballet Rambert.

The company, founded by Marie Rambert, changed its name in 1987 to Rambert Dance Company.

Christopher Bruce produced his first piece of choreography, entitled *George Frideric*, in 1969 using contemporary dance as his style. From 1975 to 1979, he was associate director at the Rambert Dance Company and in 1979 he became associate choreographer. He created about 20 works during this time. Some of the most famous are *Cruel Garden* (with Lindsay Kemp) in 1977, *Ghost Dances* in 1981 and *Sergeant Early's Dream* in 1984.

Bruce also created works for other companies and started to become well known internationally. He left the Rambert Dance

Company in 1987 and became a freelance choreographer. From 1986 to 1991, he was associate choreographer for English National Ballet, for whom he created *Swansong* in 1987. In 1991 he created *Rooster* for the Geneva Ballet.

Context and influences

Bruce's early experience at the Benson Stage Academy in ballet, tap and acrobatic dancing would always have an effect on his work, but it was when he joined Ballet Rambert that he came across other forms that would prove to be hugely influential.

Marie Rambert instilled in Bruce a need for theatricality and theatrical presentation, and this is evident in his later work, which contains strong performance images. Bruce himself worked in the theatre and observed the methods actors use. He is interested in creating a piece of theatre that engages an audience and sees his work as a form of directed drama, in which the movement performs the function of the script.

Martha Graham

When Bruce joined Ballet Rambert, the company was in the process of changing its emphasis (and subsequently its name). Associate director Norman Morrice had brought back new techniques after spending a year in America, and American choreographer Glen Tetley started to work with the company. Bruce was influenced by Tetley. No longer a **classically** based unit, it began to embrace other styles of dance. They started to experiment with a combination of ballet and modern dance and favoured the technique of Martha Graham as an influence in this.

Martha Graham is remembered for **flexed** rather than pointed feet, contractions in the stomach which begin the movement, sharp-edged movement and lots of **floor work**. In other words, the **torso**, knees and elbows come into contact with the floor and become weight-bearing.

Bruce became famous for his performances of *Pierrot Lunaire*, choreographed by Glen Tetley. It was in some ways an acrobatic work with an impressive structure on stage around which Bruce moved.

Thematic inspirations

Social messages are very important in Bruce's work. He is interested in political and environmental issues, in humanity and how people are oppressed. His pieces have a specific stimulus that has inspired him, such as Nelson Mandela's release for *Waiting* or the decadence and fall of the Weimar republic for *Berlin Requiem*, but at the same time Bruce endeavours to make their messages universal. He wants the issues he tackles to be ones the majority of people would be concerned about if they were made aware of them. His work is therefore dramatic and often emotive, having a profound effect on the audience.

Elements of the performing arts

Bruce takes his influences from a variety of sources, not just from other dance forms. This variety is the basis for the mixture of styles evident in his work.

Further study

The education department at the Rambert Dance Company has resource packs on many of Bruce's works. See what you can find out about works other than the one you are studying in detail.

Further study

Using the Internet or an encyclopedia, find out more about these two political events.

The lighthearted aspect of **vaudeville** and its wide variety of performers – from contortionists, jugglers and acrobats to singers, comedians and actors – appealed to Bruce. Similarly, the influence of music hall – the British equivalent of American vaudeville – consisting of a variety of acts and styles including song, dance and pantomime, is evident in much of his work.

Another form that was important to Bruce is **commedia dell'arte**, a type of comedy very popular in the 16th and 17th centuries that involved stock characters and set jokes or tricks, such as those in pantomime. Bruce often draws on the clowning techniques of commedia dell'arte. The white-faced clown in *Hurricane*, for example, draws on this tradition.

Clowning was also a key feature in Glen Tetley's *Pierrot Lunaire*, which Bruce became famous for performing and which used music that had itself drawn on commedia dell'arte.

Bruce also seems to have been influenced by American musical theatre and particularly by the song and dance routines of Gene Kelly and Fred Astaire, who became famous for their intricate and entertaining tap routines.

Staging

Bruce's sets are usually quite bare, with just a few necessary props, and they are not intended to be realistic. This allows the dancers plenty of space to move in so that the audience can focus on the dance itself. Similarly the lighting tends to be simplistic, creating mood or symbolic meaning.

Costume is often realistic and can reflect character and status, though often with a feeling of universality – for example, uniforms may suggest a military theme but no regime in particular.

Styles of dance

Bruce uses a mixture of classical and contemporary styles, influenced by his early training in ballet, tap, acrobatic dancing and the methods of Graham. He often adds other styles as appropriate to the subject matter of the piece, including **folk** dance, **soft-shoe** and **tango**.

Bruce sometimes mixes jazz dance styles with tap. Jazz is characterised by dancing off the beat, contractions of the stomach, more **staccato** movement (lacking the flow of ballet), bold hand gestures and lightheartedness. There is often a lower centre of gravity and feet can be parallel rather than turned out as in ballet. The arms are often used to create jagged shapes rather than curved ones as in ballet.

Movement content

Bruce experiments with movement in his work and builds his own movement vocabulary to suit his purpose. Music and its role within the performance became gradually more important to Bruce as he developed his work. In his early pieces, the movement deliberately didn't rely on music and avoided responding to it; for some productions, the music was added once the dance had been completed. However, in his later works, Bruce gave the music more significance, choosing the scores used and responding to compositions.

Further study

For more on technique, try a simple guide, such as the *Usborne Guide to Dance* by Lucy Smith (Usborne 1987).

Bruce often uses intricate footwork, circles, swirls, scooping movements and chain patterns, as well as step sequences that move in a sideways direction. Bold, circular gestures are often contrasted with small quick steps. He has invented new steps and includes folk elements such as parallel feet, **heel-to-toe** steps and a low centre of gravity. He is famous for using a flexible torso and spiralling moments.

Bruce uses a variety of relationships between dancers, from solo to ensemble. The relationships are thematically based or character based. The character is usually representative of a social class or universal character, and they generally do not have names.

Structure and form

Structure refers to the way in which the practitioner organises materials within his work and the various effects his organisation produces. Bruce's work is often broken up into different sections, scenes or episodes, which will frequently have different music. The sections will link together either thematically or in a way that constructs an overall narrative but this will not necessarily be **linear**. There might be several sections put together in one act so that the piece is unbroken by an interval. Silence is sometimes used between scenes to break up the flow of the narrative or to intensify an atmosphere, or to allow the audience to focus on the fate of a character.

The endings of Bruce's pieces are often left open to interpretation. This is linked to his reluctance to provide programme notes for the audience, leaving them able to make up their minds for themselves about what they see.

Swansong

Swansong was created for London Festival Ballet (now known as English National Ballet). It was premiered at the Teatro Arriaga, Bilbao in Spain in 1987 with the Spanish title *El Canto de Cisne*. Rambert Dance Company first performed the piece at the Theatre Royal in Norwich in 1995. Bruce was in charge of the design, while the lighting was by David Mohr. Philip Chambon composed the music, which is available on CD from Rambert Dance Company.

The piece is 32 minutes long and it is cast for three dancers: two guards and a victim. It is still sometimes performed and if you are lucky you may be able to see the piece live on stage. Watching the video is of course very helpful, but the only way to get the full impact of the piece is to see it live. If you can't see *Swansong*, then look out for performances of other works choreographed by Bruce.

Bruce was very much concerned with and inspired by the work of Amnesty International and concept of the 'prisoner of conscience'. For *Swansong*, he used two key sources:

➤ The experiences of the Chilean poet Victor Jara, under the junta of the 1970s in Chile.

➤ A novel entitled *A Man* by Oriana Fallaci, which describes the torture of its hero, Alexander Panagoulis, who was condemned to death in 1968 for attempting to assassinate the Greek dictator George Papadopoulos. He spent three and a half years in a cell.

It's also worth considering the title of the piece here: there is a long tradition that before a swan dies, it sings. Bruce was trying to make a difficult decision about the two parts of his career – as a performer and as a choreographer. *Swansong* can be seen as his

---

Bruce does not use the classical corps de ballet, with an ensemble of ballet dancers and principal dancers who take the lead roles in the narrative.

Further study

Swansong and the Houston Ballet's *Ghost Dances* can be purchased on video (2065-VI) from www.dancebooks.co.uk.

The cast can be three men or three women. Bruce stated that there could not be a combination with guards of one gender and a victim of another; a mixed cast would have to have a male and a female interrogator.

Context and influences

This also applies to *Ghost Dances* – see page 62.

Further study

If you choose to study *Swansong*, you should attempt to read Fallaci's work: see *A Man* (Simon and Schuster 1981). Make sure you are also aware of the events of 1970s Chile. Costa Gavras' film *Missing* (1982) may help.

struggle to leave his performing career behind him and continue in the future as a choreographer and thus it can be seen as his last dance before he retired as a performer.

There are seven sections in *Swansong*. The victim never leaves the stage during these, but the guards exit and enter and tap out questions. These help to link the sections together into what might be considered a narrative: there is some idea of a story being told.

1.   **Questions and answers**. The interrogators use tap to ask the victim questions and he is supposed to respond. The mood changes and the music and sound effects are used to aid this change. Trios, duets and brief solos are used to establish relationships in this section: for instance, a short tap routine at the beginning establishes the team of interrogators.

2.   **Tea for two**. Soft-shoe and tango are used and the victim has to join in. The interrogators are playing with the victim and exhausting him.

3.   **First solo**. An immediate contrast is set up as the victim performs a solo and the audience feels that there might be some respite for him. The style changes and the movements performed are more lyrical. The solo is demanding to perform as it uses a low centre of gravity in many of the movements. The balances and pliés are challenging: they are often held for a long time and require strength in the leg muscles and a good sense of balance. There are contrasts between the slow, held balletic movements and the fast steps, which walk in a very small circle to show constriction. Some of the floor work is very intricate and the pacing is important as it shifts from slow to fast and back again. There are sharp changes of direction.

Birdlike movement of the arms suggests wings in flight, and the arms are also used to imitate a bird on the ground with the feet fixed to the spot. The floor work is characteristic of contemporary dance and reflects Bruce's training in Graham technique. Formal ballet movements such as **attitudes**, **arabesques** and **jetés** are mixed with more contemporary movements such as off-balances. There are moments of suspension when a reach or arabesque is held until the dancer seems to fall into the next moment. The weight is transferred to start the next movement.

4.   **Slow trio**. The chair is pulled away from the victim and more violence and aggression is implied. There is a change of pace here as the victim is lifted and his secure base, the chair, is constantly put out of his reach. The force of the team of interrogators is gaining strength over the victim.

5.   **Second solo performed without accompaniment**. The victim performs a solo that has repetitions of certain motifs, such as arabesques, from the first solo. The chair becomes more significant here, taking several symbolic meanings.

6.   **Cane dance**. The interrogators use canes for their soft-shoe dance. Movements from other section are used, reminding the audience of past actions. The section ends with the victim collapsing and his body being placed on the chair.

Structure and form

Break it down

Work through each section, noting how the guards enter and exit. Pause the video to draw key movements and formations. What do you feel is particularly striking about each section? Note down the type of music or sound effects heard.

Think about...

How do the dancers show that the victim is learning new steps and becoming more anxious? How is violence suggested? List the movements that are particularly aggressive.

Think about...

Which movements show a desire for freedom? What do you imagine the stretching of the arm represents? How are contractions in the body used to express emotion? Which emotions?

Map the solo

Draw a rectangle for the stage area and mark the chair with a cross. Shade an area to represent the shaft of light. Draw a circle to show the dancer and trace his pathways.

Elements of the performing arts

7. **Third and final solo – interrogators on stage**. The interrogators take up their positions from section one and look at the chair as the victim performs the third and last solo. Does this imply that the victim has died and they are looking at his dead body on the chair? If so, who is dancing? Where the solo has links with the first two solos, using some of the same motifs, this solo has more birdlike movement and the victim moves closer towards the shaft of light. He travels on the diagonal towards the light and to freedom. The ambiguity of the ending is typical of Bruce.

As in other works by Bruce, the **set** of *Swansong* is very bare so that the audience's attention is not distracted from the performers. It could be anywhere in the world, and this gives the piece a universal theme, reminding the audience that people can be imprisoned anywhere.

Bruce uses the set carefully to recreate the feeling of entrapment and the smallness of the environment for the prisoner. If you look at the pathways of the guards and of the victim, you'll notice that only the guards have the freedom to come and go as they please.

The **lighting** is important in the creation of the cell and the effect of an interrogation. There is lighting above the area where the chair is positioned. David Mohr designed the lighting to be simple but very effective. The single source of light comes from high upstage left and might represent a window. The shaft of light is apparent only in the victim's solos.

The key **prop** in *Swansong* is the chair. The victim is seen sitting on it in section one and it is used throughout the piece for various purposes. Sometimes the victim wants to hold on to the chair and at other times he seems trapped by it – it could be seen to represent Bruce's dancing career. Sometimes it appears to be the victim's security, a safe haven, as he can rest on it between the periods of exhaustion.

The use of props such as the canes and red nose adds to the use of humour in the piece, but the comic aspects are double-edged, as there is a serious message behind them. The canes are used for soft-shoe dancing but later become weapons against the victim.

A characteristic feature of Bruce's work is a mix of styles and forms and this is evident in *Swansong*. The sheer variety in this piece reflects Bruce's fascination for vaudeville and music hall. He enjoys the comedy and the lighthearted approach of the artists from that style of theatre. Like a contortionist, the victim is tied in knots both mentally and physically by the two interrogators, and he is teased and tormented by their clown-like antics.

There is a theatrical element in *Swansong* that reflects Bruce's training with Marie Rambert. The dancers' facial expressions are important in the piece and communicate a great deal to the audience. The timing of the exits and entrances has also been carefully considered and the victim's reaction each time the guards come back is crucial.

Bruce has said that the style of presentation in *Swansong* is similar to that used in commedia dell'arte, in which performers became stock characters and improvisation was employed. The pieces seemed humorous but had serious messages for the audience. Bruce employs elements of commedia dell'arte and was especially influenced by the way clowns can provide a commentary of the times. In fact, he had initially thought to use clowns to perform the piece, and although he rejected this idea, some elements of clowning have been retained, such as the red nose and some of the movement. When creating *Swansong*, Bruce had the idea of using slapstick and black comedy to convey some of his message.

The interrogators use various styles of dance against the victim, to tease and humiliate him. One of these is the soft-shoe shuffle, which the audience might associate with Fred Astaire. In *Swansong*, however, it is used not to entertain the audience in a lighthearted manner, but as part of the interrogation process, and the front of the stage is amplified to pick up the soft-shoe taps and shuffles. Bruce sets up a contrast between the movement of the guards and that of the victim. He uses open arm gestures that link to the movement of a swan.

When Bruce started to choreograph *Swansong*, he was not working with any **music**. It was only after Philip Chambon came to watch Bruce working with the dancers that a successful collaboration took place, with the music and sound effects produced specially for the piece.

Chambon worked from Bruce's suggestions. For example, Bruce sang *Tea for Two* for that section and Chambon constructed a melody with the same rhythm. Bruce wanted a Latin American feel later on and so Chambon used panpipe notes in the last solo. Listen out for the changes in mood created by the changes in the music. There are moments of silence in the piece. These are interrupted by the sound of the dancer on the floor or the chair being dragged across the floor. How do we hear the soft-shoe dance and the taps? Where are they amplified? In what way are these taps forming words, questions and answers?

In some sections of the piece, there is a strong direct correlation of the dance with the music. This means that the choreography relates to the rhythm of the music. This is true of the 'Tea for Two' section, which is in syncopated $\frac{4}{4}$ time like a tango, a Latin American dance. Contrasted with this are sections in which the dancer moves away from the counts of the music and performs in a freer sense. This is particularly true of the silent sections.

Chambon used acoustic sounds, such as the metal pans in his kitchen, that were then digitally sampled. He deliberately chose to avoid electronic sounds. Metallic sounds are contrasted with the softer sounds of the wind and the flutes/panpipes used in the victim's solos to show his spirit and battle. Chambon manipulated vocal sounds to produce the cry of a bird. He used more vocal sounds to produce the 'ch-p-cha' rhythmic sound, and to make it sound slightly comic, in keeping with the vaudeville style of this section of dance.

Philip Chambon took part in the International Dance Course for Professional Choreographers and Composers as a musician in 1981. In 1984 the course was led by Christopher Bruce and Carlos Miranda, and Chambon took part as a composer. He has worked with other choreographers including Lea Anderson and Lloyd Newson.

Think about...

There are several sound effects used which sound metallic. Consider how these create atmosphere. Watch sections without the music and then again with the music. Comment on the differences.

Ghost Dances

Ghost Dances was created for Ballet Rambert and first performed in 1981 at the Bristol Theatre Royal (Old Vic). It was revived by Rambert in 1999 at the Theatre Royal, Norwich and has been performed by several companies including Nederlands Dans Theater and Houston Ballet. The duration of *Ghost Dances*, in which the dead relive moments of their lives before passing on, is about 30 minutes and it is for a cast of 11 dancers – five women and six men.

Context and influences

Ghost Dances is dedicated to the innocent people of South America, following Pinochet's coup against the elected Allende government in Chile in 1973. Bruce met Joan Jara, whose husband had been tortured and murdered by Pinochet's forces and, greatly affected by this, he was inspired to choreograph *Ghost Dances*. The piece represents the suffering that innocent people had to go through, but also their defiance and courage in enduring the violence and persecution.

Structure and form

Ghost Dances is a one-act dance, made up of seven sections, the first and last of which have the same name. The climax is in the sixth section, which involves all the dead.

1.   **Ojos Azules** (blue eyes). The three ghost dancers glide and slither across the stage using powerful movements, sometimes in canon and sometimes in unison or independently. When the music begins they perform a chain dance in a line. The dead enter from upstage and the ghost dancers appear to walk through them (shown by a contraction in the stomach).

2.   **Huajira** (a folk lament). A sextet for three men and three women performing in two trios. Unison work is prominent. The dance is animated with small steps that develop into heavier movements. The ghost dancers throw the women to the ground and finish the dance with the women before killing them.

3.   **Dolencias** (sorrows). A duet between a man in a suit and a woman in red. Her swinging arms indicate sorrow and there is much travelling. The man lifts the woman in different ways to show closeness and support. The man is lifted in the air by the ghost dancers and we see his legs moving as he dies.

4.   **Papel de Plata** (silver paper). A peasant boy dances alone and is then accompanied by female dancers. The steps are characterised by a small step executed with the heel touching the floor first. There are small jumps. A man dances with three of the women and is then led away by a ghost dancer.

5.   **Mis Llamitas** (evokes the walk of the llama). A man in a white shirt dances with a woman in a white dress. The man's tie is used by the woman to lead him while he performs movements reminiscent of a llama. The man's movement becomes more powerful as he moves away from the woman. The dance is playful and light-hearted until the woman jumps up for a second piggy-back from the man but falls into the arms of a ghost dancer, indicating death.

6.   **Sicuriadas** (a traditional dance tune). The dead come in two by two and repeat some of the earlier movements. The pairs perform in unison one after the other, then two lines of four dancers perform movements which become faster and faster.

7.   **Ojos Azules** (blue eyes). The ghost dancers come out from behind the rocks. There is a sense of circularity as the ghost dancers return to movements from the beginning of the piece. The dead form a procession with their eyes fixed ahead. The ghost dancers return to their opening positions and one has the feeling that the whole event is about to start again with new people.

The **music** is by a Chilean group called Inti-Illimani, who Bruce met in 1979, and it is important in helping to divide the piece into sections. Bruce took six numbers from the recording *Canto de Pueblos Andinos*, which comprised two songs and four folk tunes. Bruce wanted the music to be played live and research had to be carried out into the special instruments used: bombo, charango, guitarrone, quena, sikus and tiple. The musicians of the Mercury Ensemble had to learn to play the instruments and sing in Spanish.

Bruce himself was responsible for the **set design** for *Ghost Dances*. He asked set painter John Campbell to base it on a photograph of an Andean view. Created for a **proscenium arch** stage, the set has a painted backcloth representing the mouth of a cave. There are rocklike structures on stage, giving the ghost dancers more levels on which to work.

The **costume design** was by Belinda Scarlett. She watched the rehearsals of the piece and consulted a book given to her by Bruce, which included masks of the natives of South America. The **lighting**, by Nick Chelton, is used to enhance the action and to change the mood. The lighting changes are generally slow, apart from when sudden deaths occur. Shadows are created and there is a green wash over the set, making it gloomy and sinister. Side lighting helps to show the definition of the ghost dancers' bodies.

In terms of **movement**, when you watch the piece for the first time, the images of the ghost dancers in their skeletal costumes will haunt you. The skull-like faces and ragged costumes present a striking image on stage, perhaps more so because the three ghost dancers never leave the stage. They perform animalistic movements and make themselves look like birds and reptiles. They are symbolic of dictators, military regimes, death squads and all those who have oppressed the people of South America.

The other set of characters are the dead, performed by five women and three men. Notice where they enter and exit the stage. What does the exit represent? The relationships between them are not clearly defined but the audience can recognise strong emotional bonds between certain characters. What might these be? How are they shown through dance? Why are they not clearly delineated? Look carefully at the costumes and try to decide which social class each member of the dead comes from. Bruce describes them as 'on their way to Heaven or Hell'. What does he mean?

Elements of performing arts

> **Tip**
> Watch the piece with the volume switched off so that you can concentrate on the lighting changes and how they influence or create mood.

Drawing tableaux
Look at the formations of the dancers. There are examples of many types of relationship from solo to full ensemble. Draw sketches showing tableaux of characters to help you see how sets of characters are placed on stage at different levels from one another and in different areas of the stage. Read the section on page 31.

Stylistically, there is a heavy concentration on folk dance in *Ghost Dances* which is mixed with classical ballet and Graham technique. This fusion of contemporary and classical forms is characteristic of Bruce's work. There is also a strong sense of character in the piece that demonstrates Bruce's interest in drama.

Bruce creates his own folk-inspired steps based on an understanding of the form. Some of the features involve intricate footwork, use of chain and circle formations, spinning turns and line dances that move from side to side. The use of a flexible torso and spiralling movements are characteristic of Bruce's work.

Also worth noting is the weighty, squatting movement with feet parallel and apart and arms stretched out in front. Similarly, observe the triplet with swinging arms that expresses sorrow: the feet are parallel and the body is curved forward with the head down; the hands move across the face to express sorrow.

Checklist

To make it easier for you to keep in mind what the most important features of Bruce's work are, here is a checklist of those we've discussed above. The list is not exhaustive – you may find things that you'd like to add – nor should you expect to find all of these in every work: these are simply guidelines.

- ☑ **Stimulus material** such as music, paintings and works of literature on which to base his dance pieces.
- ☑ Works convey an **ecological, political or social message**.
- ☑ **Interpretation** remains open – Bruce does not give out any programme notes.
- ☑ Message is often **universal** and concerns human suffering.
- ☑ Bruce uses a **fusion of dance techniques**, generally ballet and contemporary. The technique of Martha Graham is clearly an influence as he trained with her. He uses other dance styles such as folk and social dancing, tap and flamenco. He takes the essence of the style and creates his own steps and movements. Bruce uses **gesture** in his work.
- ☑ The works are **thematic** and **episodic** rather than strictly narrative.
- ☑ There is often a strong sense of **character**.
- ☑ **Music** plays a significant role in the structuring of the piece and in giving it a particular flavour.
- ☑ Bruce has a strong **visual sense** which extends beyond the choreography and includes the set, lighting and costumes. Bruce does not want the stage set to interfere with the dance and sets are often bare as costumes are free-flowing or able to stretch easily so as not to impede the movement.

Lloyd Newson

Lloyd Newson's work has been both adored and abhorred. It is challenging, often shocking, and can be very difficult to analyse. His pieces are not for the faint-hearted and you should think carefully before making the decision to study his work. The movement is explicit, often sexually so, and very aggressive. It demands high levels of strength, stamina and energy in performance, and requires performers to be prepared to expose the truth about human behaviour. However, it is for these very reasons that Newson is a highly interesting choreographer to study.

> **Tip**
>
> When you begin studying a piece of dance, try to find out details about all the people who worked on it, such as the composer of the music, the lighting designer, the set designer and the costume designer.

Context and influences

Born in Australia in 1957, Newson did not develop his interest in dance until he was a student studying for a degree in psychology. His first dancing job was in 1979 with the New Zealand Ballet. He came to Britain in 1980 and danced with Extemporary Dance Theatre from 1981 to 1985. Newson made two works for Extemporary, entitled *Breaking Images* (1982) and *Beauty, Art and the Kitchen Sink* (1984), which indicated clearly that he wanted to challenge stereotypes in the dance world and break down barriers. Then in 1986, Newson formed DV8 with Nigel Charnock and Michelle Richecoeur. They were later joined by Liz Ranken.

The name DV8 refers to the Video-8 camera that was used during rehearsals of *Strange Fish* – partly to record all the movements made by the performers, whether consciously or unconsciously. The camera was used as part of the creative process. DV8 can also be seen to stand for 'deviate' and reflects how Newson deviates from what is considered the norm of dance.

See pages 68–70 for a detailed analysis of *Strange Fish*.

Newson's background in psychology goes some way to explaining his interest in relationships between people and the intricate behaviour that men and women display in getting to know each other. He is well known for his non-conformist approach to dance and his wish to reflect human desires and needs through dance and physical theatre. He started DV8 in order to explore more political and challenging ideas, and he will only work on a project when he has something new to say.

Human relationships

Newson is known for his treatment of taboo subjects that challenge the audience to think about what they are seeing. For example, *Dead Dreams of Monochrome Men* (1988) is about necrophilia and homosexual murder. The starting point for this piece was Brian Master's study of Dennis Nilsen, *Killing for Company*, which tells the life story of Nilsen, a mass murderer who described himself as a 'monochrome man'. The themes that run through the piece are loneliness, aggression and despair.

Taboo subjects

Necrophilia is an obsession with death and dead bodies, often involving sexual attraction to corpses.

Killing for Company: the case of Dennis Nilsen by Brian Masters (Arrow 1995).

One of DV8's first pieces was a collaboration between Lloyd Newson and Nigel Charnock entitled *My Sex Our Dance* (1986), which looks at a male relationship. It shows violence and aggression in extreme movement terms and could easily shock an audience. This is one of the striking features of Newson's work. It may not set out to shock an audience on purpose, but the extreme version of honesty witnessed on the stage is certainly an eye-opener for many who have not encountered his work before.

> **Further study**
>
> Newson's style or approach has been likened to that of German choreographer Pina Bausch, as it is non-narrative and it is highly dramatic and emotional. See what you can find out about the work of Bausch.

eye-opener for many who have not encountered his work before. Newson's reason for using such tactics is that he wants to educate and inform his audience, to make them aware of issues in society and to make them form their own opinions.

Newson seems to enjoy presenting gender stereotypes and making the audience aware of the ridiculous nature of competition between people. In *Enter Achilles*, for example, he shows us men in a pub trying to be macho and fighting over a pint of beer.

The philosophy of DV8

Web link

There are a lot of useful resources, including DV8's artistic policy and interviews with Newson, at www.dv8.co.uk.

'Cottaging' refers to homosexual activity between men in public toilets.

> ❝ I got to a point where so many choreographers denied who I was, my ideas, my thought, and I was nothing more than a bit of pigment for them to paint with; and the reality is dancers are *not* pigment. They are living and feeling, and you can't deny, no matter how you try, the humanity on stage. ❞
>
> Newson, *Dance & Dancers*, July 1992.

DV8 Physical Theatre, described by those involved as 'an independent collective of dancers' (indicating that they regard one another as equals) came together because its members had 'become frustrated and disillusioned with the preoccupation and direction of most dance'. They describe the work of DV8 as being 'about taking risks, aesthetically and physically, about breaking down the barriers between dance, theatre and personal politics and, above all, communicating ideas and feelings clearly and unpretentiously. It is determined to be radical yet accessible, and to take its work to as wide an audience as possible.'

Newson's approach to creating a piece is to assemble the company when a new work is to be made and to choose dancers who are suited to the subject matter and themes of the piece. The company is constantly changing in order to meet the demands of the pieces. Newson wants his performers to be honest and truthful and to create physical truth that is drawn from personal experience. In order to achieve this truth in performance, the dancers will undertake preparatory work to prepare them – for example, dancers in *MSM* (1993) visited cottaging locations. Newson says that he does not want his performers to be 'obedient bodies' and he never imposes movement on the dancers, since he believes that they should have choices and should be able to contribute to the creative process. He has participated in much of his own work as a dancer and choreographer, and he will often bring in specialist teachers – for example, a yoga teacher, an Irish-dance teacher or a voice coach – to help the performers gain the appropriate skills for the piece.

Newson does not always choose dancers with ostensibly perfect bodies, those who usually audition for ballet companies. He doesn't care about the age, the weight or the height of his dancers, and has worked with both able-bodied and disabled dancers to create pieces such as *Can We Afford This/The Cost of Living*. In *Bound to Please*, he has a 67-year-old woman naked on stage and kissing a younger man. He sees beauty as the breadth of human experience and does not believe that dance should be about one type of beauty.

Structure and form

Structure in Newson's work is generally **episodic** and might appear abstract, though it usually has a sense of narrative, or is sometimes based around the idea that a character goes on a journey. Newson is not keen on beginning to work on a new piece with no structure at all set out in advance, but nor does he want to be constrained by a very rigid pre-determined structure. He often writes a scenario or loose structure before they begin the rehearsals, so that he has something with which to work, but is more than willing to diverge from this during the rehearsals.

Between their productions, it seems that DV8's policy is to experiment and then only come together when they find that they have something to say through physical theatre. They tend to start with very simple ideas of what they want to convey; the rest comes together as they work on the piece. In an interview, Newson explained how variable the process can be:

> The material comes from many different ways, there is no set rule. Sometimes I will come in and I will have a vague idea — it might be one little sentence and you improvise on that for three hours. It might be that one day I was on a bus, waiting to get off, and I noticed people watching me and I started getting anxious and twitching a little bit, and I had to try and pretend I wasn't and they kept looking at me. Other times, it might be as simple as that I woke up one day with someone's arm across me, and I panicked because I thought is this trapped, or is this embraced? And I liked the ambiguity or duality.

Newson might start with the idea of a set, and in some ways this helps start the structure of the work.

Web link

Interview in *Dance and Dancers*, July 1992. Also available at www.dv8.co.uk/press/interviews/strangeFish.html

Elements of the performing arts

It is important to notice that the company calls itself DV8 Physical Theatre, since this indicates their attempt to move away from more traditional types of dance and to incorporate other forms such as drama in their work.

Physical theatre

Physical theatre embraces all types of movement and is not a codified language of movement as such. It's easier to understand this concept if you consider how in ballet, the dancer has to learn set moves from a young age and practise them until they are performed perfectly. All the moves learned are put together into a language of movement – they are part of a distinct vocabulary.

In physical theatre, it is more difficult to name set moves because that is exactly the opposite of what the dancers want to achieve. The policy of DV8 is to create moves that are necessary to convey emotion and messages. The movement will come from the dancer and be original. They do not want to reinforce 'accepted values and traditions'. If you think about what is traditional in dance, you may imagine thin women dressed in tutus, dancing gracefully on a proscenium arch stage. DV8 stand against the idea that females must form the **corps de ballet** and that only a few dancers can have central roles in the piece.

> In their manifesto, DV8 declare themselves to be against 'the concept of dance restricted to a set vocabulary of movement and concerns'.

One of the traits of Newson's work is that the performers push themselves to extremes. For example, in *Dead Dreams of Monochrome Men*, one performer flings himself from a high wall into his partner's arms. This scene is echoed later, with the same man being treated badly and thrown to the floor. What the audience witnesses on stage is not the aesthetically pleasing images of ballet – it is not the unison work of a well-rehearsed chorus, nor the highly acclaimed technique of the **prima ballerina** with beautiful costumes and set. Instead the audience is bombarded by aggressive and often ugly movements that expose the thoughts and emotions of the characters on stage.

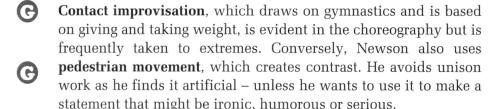 **Contact improvisation**, which draws on gymnastics and is based on giving and taking weight, is evident in the choreography but is frequently taken to extremes. Conversely, Newson also uses **pedestrian movement**, which creates contrast. He avoids unison work as he finds it artificial – unless he wants to use it to make a statement that might be ironic, humorous or serious.

Staging Newson uses a range of media for his pieces and has unusual sets – a pub in *Enter Achilles*, a specially constructed green grassy slope in *Can We Afford This/The Cost of Living*, and public toilets in *MSM*. The sets represent real life – the dancers perform not on a proscenium arch stage but in a site-specific space. The set for *Strange Fish* is elaborate, with water under floorboards playing a significant role.

For *Dead Dreams of Monochrome Men*, the setting changes from a street to a pub to a house, and takes the audience on a journey through eroticism, murder and manipulative sex. The set includes walls that conceal ladders, a Venetian blind and a bathtub against a wall with a mirror. The images are disturbing and have even prompted critics to ask whether this is dance at all.

Indeed, as indicated by the term physical theatre, DV8's work is about far more than just dance. Newson frequently introduces songs, dialogue and soundscapes to add to the pieces. He does not work within traditional boundaries but uses whatever he thinks will work for a particular performance. For example, in *Enter Achilles* there is a scene in which a man is having sex with a blow-up doll when his girlfriend rings up. He does not pick up the phone so she leaves a message while he continues to concentrate on the doll. It conveys that he is rejecting a potentially real relationship with another human being for one with a plastic substitute.

Strange Fish

Strange Fish was first performed in Budapest on 25 April 1992 and had its British premiere on 9 June 1992 at the Tramway in Glasgow. The stage version is 90 minutes long and the video around 35. The dancing cast was composed of Wendy Houston, who played the central character, Lauren Potter, Jordi Cortes Molina, Nigel Charnock, Kate Champion and Dale Tanner. They were accompanied by 64-year-old Diana Payne-Myers and singer Melanie Pappenheim. The music was composed by Jocelyn Pook.

When DV8 started working on this piece they had few expectations. Although they had done a lot of preparatory work, they didn't know what the end product would be. The initial concept seems to have come from ideas about loss of faith as well as how people feel about themselves and their relationships with others. The rest appears to have been developed through the improvisation process, in which Newson built on the individual characteristics and qualities of the performers.

Further study

Strange Fish PAL Video (2673-VI) is available to order from www.dancebooks.co.uk.

In many ways, *Strange Fish* marks a departure from Newson's previous work. Newson was keen to move away from the intense **physicality** of his earlier pieces, such as *Dead Dreams*, and in *Strange Fish*, there is much use of humour and entertainment to convey the messages of the piece. Rather than the stark **realism** of previous pieces, *Strange Fish* is full of surrealism and absurdism. The importance of the set (discussed *below*) to the overall piece is demonstrated by the fact that Newson had the set built before the movement content was put together. This meant that the performers could get to know the set right from the beginning and it could influence the development of the movement as the piece was created.

The title was chosen after someone referred to Charnock as a 'strange fish', though it fits the piece in many other ways. It suits the water imagery and the way the piece ends. The water can represent many things, from the ideas of humans evolving from creatures in the sea to the unconscious mind.

Strange Fish comprises a number of scenes that follow on from one another. They examine the relationships between a group of men and women while tracing the journey of the central character, Wendy Houston. The piece starts with Houston in a religious setting and she seems to be questioning her faith. She experiences a range of emotions as she makes contact with the other dancers and explores different relationships with each of them. She is sometimes an observer and sometimes an active, if somewhat detached, participant in the various activities which ensue.

The themes running through *Strange Fish* are faith, belief, expectation, anticipation, disappointment, desire for friendship and to be included, isolation and loneliness. In Newson's own words, the piece 'is about friendship and about the search for something or someone to believe in. It looks at how misunderstandings affect our relationships and how in turn these begin to influence what we ultimately believe. It questions whether our need for love and intimacy saves or enslaves us. Is it a lack of belief in ourselves that drives us to place our hopes in things beyond our immediate lives? The need to maintain faith and belief often distorts perception: through anticipation and expectation we create situations in our minds that can never match reality and by doing so perpetuate dissatisfaction with what life has to offer.'

In the programme for *Strange Fish*, Newson included the Buddhist saying 'Be as ignorant of what you want to catch as the fisherman is of what is at the end of his line' – in other words, telling us to expect nothing. In *Strange Fish*, Houston expects people to perform the impossible: she wants Tanner to stand in a handstand for longer than is reasonably possible. She can only be disappointed if she adopts this attitude.

The **set** for *Strange Fish*, designed by Peter J. Davison, is designed to look like a church decorated with candles. It also contains many surprises, such as floorboards that can be lifted up to show water underneath and pebbles that are used for stoning. The set is active in that it plays a key role in the dancers' movements as they perform on it, against it and under it.

Structure and form

Breaking it down

Go through the piece scene by scene, noting down the key details of each character's relationship to the others.

Web link

Lloyd Newson quoted at: www.dv8.co.uk/strangefish/fish.folder.html.

Elements of performing arts

The video shows the set of a hall where people meet and dance and a corridor with rooms off it.

Strange Fish involves several scenes in which the **movement** is shocking but effective in communicating with the audience. The piece begins with a naked woman writhing like a snake on a cross. This image in itself would be shocking to some members of the audience as it posits the figure as a woman Christ figure who could therefore be viewed as an impostor, an intruder and a sacrilege. The movement that follows seems to be part of a ritual. An audience might see this scene as anti-religious, but Newson claims that it can be read in almost the opposite sense. At the end, Houston has lost friends and faith. Her loss of faith is represented by her going up to the figure on the cross and having the life sucked out of her, leaving her crumpled up on the floor.

In another potentially shocking scene, Houston is portrayed having a one-night stand with a male dancer. She moves herself away from under his sexually engaged body, which is moving intently up and down on top of her. What's shocking here is that he doesn't seem to notice her absence and just continues on his own.

A contrasting sex scene takes place between Potter and Cortes Molina, in which their movement shows them to be completely devoted to each other. Their bodies move fluidly around each other on a bench, giving the impression that they are entangled. Newson asked them to improvise starting with the idea of hands being clasped and making their bodies clasp each other. There is an ambiguity in the movement, as it looks intimate but could also indicate entrapment. Houston tries to get between them because she feels left out, just as Charnock does among the group that forms couples. He flings himself at them and tries to worm his way into their relationships in a disturbing manner that displays no shame.

It is unusual to find **words and dialogue** in a dance piece but it is typical of Newson to use whichever medium seems appropriate to the piece. Charnock, for example, delivers a frenetic **monologue** about having friends, when he clearly has none. In the scene with the blond wig, Houston and Potter giggle a great deal when they try to get the attention of a man, a gender stereotype typical of Newson.

Checklist

Here is a basic list of Newson's fingerprints. Which apply to the piece you are studying?

- ☑ **Challenging** for the audience and often **shocking**, deliberately targeting **taboo subjects**
- ☑ **Physically demanding** movement, with performers often taking **risks**
- ☑ **Physical theatre**, consciously challenging the formal and established conventions of traditional dance forms
- ☑ Reflects **human needs and desires**, and explores **human relationships**
- ☑ Works put together through **improvisation** and **experimentation**
- ☑ **Unusual sets** which performers work with from early stage
- ☑ Use of **songs**, **dialogue**, **soundscapes**.

Bertolt Brecht

There has probably been more written about German dramatist Bertolt Brecht (1898–1956) than any other playwright of the 20th century. As a poet, theorist, playwright and director, he casts a giant shadow and has been a major influence on many significant theatre practitioners and playwrights across the world. However, as a subject of study, he tends to suffer from theoretical overload and a lot of misunderstanding. Indeed, he wrote so much that there is not space to do real justice to the development of his theoretical views. While the theory is important, you must always remember that essentially Brecht is a dramatist, a maker of plays. Sometimes the plays don't seem to reflect the theory, and in later life Brecht felt the pressure of being expected to conform to his own theory.

Context of Brecht's work

For a real understanding of the context in which Brecht was working, you need to have a good grasp of what had gone before him in terms of theatre history. Brecht was reacting against the form and content of plays. The advent of realism (sometimes referred to as 'naturalism') within European theatre had made Brecht determined to change the place of theatre within society. He wanted to change the attitude of the audience towards what they saw on the stage: German audiences were mainly bourgeois (middle-class) and took theatre very seriously, viewing it as an art form, with their role as passive onlookers. Brecht wished to make theatre popular, relevant and accessible to all.

Brecht's driving concern for a theatre that is entertaining and artistic but also instructional permeates most of his middle and late work, but is evident as early as *The Threepenny Opera* (1928).

Brecht was born in Augsburg, Germany to a fairly affluent family. Having studied medicine at university, Brecht worked briefly in an army hospital during the first world war. The horrific nature of what he saw there led him to develop strong feelings against war and against the bourgeois classes.

The years between the first and second world wars in Germany were a time of huge inflation – thanks to the punitive reparations placed on Germany after the first world war – as well as poverty, unemployment and political unrest, with the repercussions of the Bolshevik Revolution being felt across Europe. It is unclear whether Brecht was involved in the various political uprisings, but *Drums in the Night* was based on the left-wing Spartacus Rising in Berlin in 1919. Four years later, Hitler would lead an uprising in Munich that failed, but the seeds of national socialism were already set in a fertile ground.

In 1924, Brecht moved to Berlin, where he continued to develop his interest in Marxism and became very outspoken against the Nazi party. With the advent of a Nazi government in 1933, he was forced into exile and went to live in first Denmark, then America, before returning to Germany in 1949. He then set up his own company, the Berliner Ensemble, and this was the work of the remaining seven years of his life.

There is much that you can find quite easily in libraries and on the Internet to expand your understanding of Brecht's plays, theory and productions, but don't feel you have to know everything about Brechtian theory. What's important is that you are able to recognise what's going on in the chosen play and that you can make a good attempt at making sense of his work.

Further reading

For more on this, see *Brecht in Context* by John Willett (Methuen 1998).

Politics and war

While much has been made of the influence on Brecht of his involvement in the first world war, in fact he served as a medical orderly in a VD ward for only a few months.

Further study

To understand Brecht's political development, his reasons for exile from Germany and the context surrounding his work in all its stages, you will need a basic grasp on world developments 1933–1955, including the politics of Nazi Germany and the Cold War.

Stylistic influences

Brecht's work can be roughly broken down into three main stages: his expressionist early plays, the Lehrstücke ('learning plays') of the 1930s and the mature parable plays of the 1940s.

Expressionist plays

Further study

See if you can find images of the work of George Grosz and Otto Dix on the Internet. Their work is some of the best German expressionist art of the period.

Expressionism was a movement in art and literature that had originated in Germany before the first world war. It was concerned with breaking down superficial ideas of reality to investigate the deeper meanings underneath. Works of art associated with this movement often appear distorted, even grotesque. Brecht's plays from this period are enthusiastic, raw, brash and grubby, with a keen sense of theatre and the audience, but they are also immature, with Brecht seeming somewhat confused in taking a position. *Baal*, his first play (1918), concerns a lad with deliberately disgusting habits and amoral outlook. We don't particularly like him but he is so disreputable that we do want to know what happens to him.

Brecht ultimately rejected Expressionism because he felt it relied too heavily on the irrational. However, Expressionism certainly influenced the way he tried to get audiences thinking about stories and theatre with a new perspective; the way he fragmented the line of his stories and created episodes; and the way he treated the characters of his plays (in that they were types of people).

Lehrstücke

In Berlin, Brecht met Erwin Piscator, with whom he shared an interest in political theatre and in using theatre as a means for political protest. It was here that he began to write his Lehrstücke, exploring the idea of teaching through drama. Written between 1928 and 1930, the plays were short **parabolic** pieces, written to instruct children. They were not very appealing to audiences since they lacked a theatrical spark. They earned Brecht the reputation of being very **didactic** – trying to use his plays to teach lessons and make points. This led to the playwright Ionesco calling him 'The Postman', as he only wanted to deliver messages. *The Measures Taken* (1930), for example, involves a young communist murdered by the Party. The freedom of the individual is sacrificed for the future freedom of mankind.

The later years

See *below* for more on epic and dialectical theatre.

While in exile, Brecht developed his ideas on epic theatre and wrote most of what are now considered to be his great plays. In these plays, the meaning is exposed through skilful, but purposeful telling of the story. These plays were **dialectic** – Brecht wanted to use scenes and situations to create an argument with all sides shown, and with the audience encouraged to play an active role in making their own mind up during the play and on leaving the theatre. The beginnings of the shift to the later stage can be seen in a lecture given in 1939 called 'On Experimental Theatre' translated in John Willett's *Brecht on Theatre*. His last play, *The Caucasian Chalk Circle,* brings together two tales as a play within a play and unusually has a happy ending.

Sporting events

The spectacle of mass entertainment at sporting events encouraged Brecht's ideas of popular theatre. He compared the experience to a boxing match, in which the audience is fully engaged in the combat. He wished to emulate sport's universal appeal.

During his working life, Brecht had the opportunity to work with some of the leading practitioners of the time, although he treated many of them abominably. Directors Max Reinhardt and Erwin Piscator, composers Weill, Eisler and Dessau, and the designer Casper Neher all worked with him. There were also the unrecognised collaborators, namely Elisabeth Hauptmann, also known as 'Dorothy Lane', the writer of *Happy End*, who is thought to have had a major (but unacknowledged because the Brecht name earned more) input into the plays.

Structure and form

'Epic theatre' was a term developed by the director Erwin Piscator, with whom Brecht worked in Berlin, but it is a concept that Brecht adopted and expanded, so that it is now mainly associated with him. Brecht created a table to indicate the shift of emphasis from Aristotelian or dramatic theatre to epic theatre. It essentially outlines a theatre that is objective and in which the audience is actively engaged. They have to **reason** about what takes place on stage, rather than simply being submissively involved. In epic theatre, the work is on a large scale and, in the same way we use 'epic' elsewhere, it creates a picture of the world through the investigation of the individual. However, this does not assume a universal human response; rather the actor, playwright and audience should understand the specific circumstances that are responsible for the character's actions in a given situation and period. Epic theatre can be achieved through a variety of means:

> **Episodic action** does not follow a chronological time pattern but consists of selected episodes in a story or journey. The time can be displaced, as in *The Caucasian Chalk Circle*, or spread over years, as in *Mother Courage*. Each episode is almost a complete dramatic entity in itself. We are told **what** will happen, but the important thing is to witness **how** it happens, which is the reason for the poems, placards, and narration at the start of a scene.

> **Montage rather than organic growth**. Ideas, action, and attitudes do not grow out of each other in the play. Rather they are layered and juxtaposed deliberately by the playwright to force the audience to think about their relevance and relationship to the story, the characters and themselves.

> **Narrative rather than plot**. Many characters go on a journey, but it is not one of self-realisation, as in a Shakespearean tragedy such as *King Lear*. It is a journey that they must take in the interests of their own survival. Mother Courage is a selfish, greedy, entrepreneur who makes destructive wars possible, but she must follow the armies for her survival.

Elements of the performing arts

Keen to ensure that his plays were performed in the way he intended, Brecht directed them himself and instructed the performers through his theory. Brecht wanted his actors to distance themselves from the characters they were playing. He created many devices to help his actors achieve this distance. He felt his actors should demonstrate rather than become a role. He saw them as storytellers who could play many parts and have a

Other art forms

See pages 75–76 for more on music and dance in Brecht's work.

Epic theatre

This is in 'The Modern Theatre is the Epic Theatre', notes to his opera *The Rise and Fall of the City of Mahagonny* written with Kurt Weill in 1930. You can find it reproduced in a number of places, including John Willett's book *Brecht on Theatre*.

Actors and the audience

view of the characters they were playing. He allowed them to step out of their emotional engagement with a character to look critically at what they represented. While his discussions of theory seem to be so concerned about ensemble playing and collective decision-making, as a director and promoter of his work, Brecht in fact comes across as having been a bit of a control freak.

Brecht wanted the audience to become part of the piece, but not in an **empathic** way. He wanted them to be active participants in the creation of the society of the play. His audiences are active witnesses to the action, rather than passive receivers undergoing a **cathartic** experience.

Dialectical theatre

Dialectics is the juxtaposition of contradictory ideas in order to arrive at the truth. Brecht uses contradictions frequently in his plays in numerous ways. In *The Good Woman of Setzuan*, in order to survive Shen Te has to create an imaginary cousin, Shui Ta, who is everything that she is not. Puntila in *Mr Puntila and His Man Matti* is kind and generous when drunk, but rude and selfish when sober. 'Terrible is the temptation to do good' says the Singer in *The Caucasian Chalk Circle*, presenting us with a contradiction that makes us sit up and think. But in a corrupt world, where those who can look out for themselves do so, and those who can't simply suffer, then the Singer is right. In a moral world, the temptation to be bad is the thing we fear most. In an immoral world, turned over by war and squabbles in the ruling class, it is doing something good that is likely to get us into trouble. Dialectics concentrates on the contradictions that exist in events and in characters, and explores them in a way that makes them more dynamic and vigorous.

Making strange

Brecht's Verfremdungseffekt, or V-effect, is often confusingly referred to as the 'alienation effect' in English. The point of it is to distance the actor and audience from emotional involvement in the drama. Unfortunately, by use of this term it is often misunderstood as 'alienating the audience', but this was the last thing Brecht wanted. Brecht sought to achieve what we would now call an interactive audience, an audience that was alert and engaged in the 'debate' before them, not submerged in a make-believe of feeling and emotion. Thus, it is not alienation *of* the audience, but *for* the audience.

Consequently, it is safer to use a literal translation of the original German: 'the effect of making strange'. The V-effect is the main vehicle for achieving epic theatre, and Brecht suggested a number of theatrical devices that continually remind the audience they are watching a play and refocus them on the issue:

> Scenes can be prefaced with an introduction. The introduction may be on a placard or projection, and tells the audience **what** is going to happen so that they concentrate on **how** it happens.

> Dialogue and action should be broken up with songs and poems that underline a point.

> The stage should not attempt to create an illusion of somewhere other than a theatre stage. It should be flooded in open white light, and the lanterns and technology of the theatre should be

Tip

When discussing Brecht's language, always keep in mind that you are reading a translation of Brecht's original German. The translator will have tried to match the style and level of the language of the original, but be careful about attributing too much significance to individual words.

exposed. Set, props and costumes should be stripped back to the essentials, but must then be authentic.

➢ Actors should be seen to change costume and take on multiple roles.

➢ Machinery should be used on stage to emphasise that it is industry. Projected images, text and film are used to assist the idea of 'montage' of attitudes and ideas.

Gestus or **Gest** is a difficult term to translate and to grasp, but is a very useful idea for performers in all art forms. It means reducing the actor's physicality in performance to an essential action or gesture that carries some definitive meaning. It involves clear and stylised body language as well as facial expression and tone of voice. Gestus helps portray the social relationships between characters rather than the psychological motivation. For Brecht, gestus was a way of characters externalising their feelings, and could also be exercised through music.

For Brecht, music was a major element of the theatre he wanted to create. He had worked as a cabaret artist when a student and for him, as with everything else, music was a means to an end. The music should have attitude as much as the characters and the costumes. He called it 'misuk' to distinguish it from the romanticism of 19th-century western composition. He wanted music that combined Stravinsky and Satie with **jazz** and blues in a cabaret-cum-operetta setting, incorporating all the new styles, but with a style of its own.

Brecht insisted the words should be dominant and clear, with the music underlining and emphasising the political intention. Having read some of his poems, Kurt Weill (1900–1950) was willing to become his first major collaborator. This famous pairing was to give us *The Threepenny Opera*, loosely based on John Gay's 18th-century play *The Beggar's Opera*, with the now-classic 'Mack the Knife'; a ballet; an opera, *The Rise and Fall of the City of Mahagonny* for full orchestra and chorus, creating an image of Berlin in the 1920s; and a music-theatre piece entitled *Happy End* with some terrific music and lyrics but an underdeveloped storyline about gangsters in America meeting a Salvation Army evangelist. The story was to appear in a different guise 20 years later in the musical *Guys and Dolls*.

Brecht then worked with Hanns Eisler (1898–1962), a pupil of Arnold Schoenberg and a committed Communist. Eisler's 'applied music' is hard and severe – Brecht called it 'more serious' and they both felt it should have at least as much effect on the performer as on the audience. They worked together in Hollywood on a Fritz Lang film *Hangmen also Die* and the American production of *The Life of Galileo*. Like all of Brecht's collaborators, Eisler was a significant practitioner himself, composing film scores; symphonic, chamber and piano music; and vocal and choral music including the collection of politicised Lieder (songs) called *The Hollywood Songbook* as well as the national anthem of East Germany.

Gestus

> One example of Gest would be a woman with her arms positioned as if she were holding a baby, with her faced turned towards the imagined baby and perhaps smiling. The audience would know immediately from this that she is a mother.

Music, poetry and politics

> Later, Weill, seeking to break from his partner's dominant and increasingly rigid approach, moved first to Paris and then to America with his wife Lotte Lenya, the distinctive voice behind the success of many of their songs, and worked with the influential left-wing drama company The Group Theatre.

Coming from the same stable as Weill and Eisler, Brecht's third collaborator, Paul Dessau (1894–1979) produced music that is spiky and aggressive. More full of character than the music of composers Brecht had worked with previously, this harsh jangling mood was less successful at underlining the words. While Dessau wrote for the later plays, there was less actual collective working together as there had been with Weill and Eisler, and little of Dessau's music has survived in the theatre performance repertory. Their most artistically successful collaboration was the ill-fated opera *The Trial of Lucullus*, rewritten at the insistence of the East German government as *The Condemnation of Lucullus* and ignored by the state press when first performed.

Dance

" First comes the sweat. Then comes the beauty – if you're very lucky and have said your prayers. "

Balanchine, quoted by Bernard Taper in *Balanchine: A Biography* (University of California Press 1996).

Despite their differences, Kurt Weill asked Brecht to write the book for a ballet with songs, *The Seven Deadly Sins of the Petty Bourgeoisie*, in 1933. This was a collaboration with the Paris company Les Ballets, led by the avant-garde choreographer and dance radical George Balanchine (1904–1983), who had already antagonised traditional ballet companies across Europe with his innovative approach to the traditional ballet style. His style was distinguished by speed and an energetic physicality, expanding the range of traditional ballet.

The piece follows the character Anna as she sets out on a seven-year journey to seven cities of a debauched and corrupt America, to earn enough to get a house for the family. It was Brecht's only major involvement with formal dance. However, informal dance appears often in the plays. *The Caucasian Chalk Circle* ends with a celebratory dance to indicate the final harmony, not unlike a Shakespearean comedy.

Caucasian Chalk Circle

Brecht likened himself to Shakespeare when criticised for taking the stories of others and re-working previous ideas of his own. Thus his last play, *The Caucasian Chalk Circle*, is a combination of two previous works – hence the two stories – and is based on Klabund's version of the Chinese play, *The Chalk Circle*. Brecht wrote the play in 1944 when he was living in America and he changed the location of the Chinese play to contemporary soviet Georgia in the Caucasus.

The part of Grusha was originally written for the Oscar-winning actress Luise Rainer at her request, and the play was to be produced on Broadway. Brecht then fell out with her and rewrote the part to make it more human and ordinary.

Form and structure

Typically of Brecht, *The Caucasian Chalk Circle* is **episodic** and jumps backwards and forwards in time. The play is made up of a **prologue** followed by five acts. The prologue follows a debate between two groups of peasants over the use of a valley. The fruit farmers, who win the valley, celebrate and the Singer agrees to tell them the story that follows – the story of the Chalk Circle. This then serves as a **play within a play**, further distancing the audience from the action. Brecht's message in *The Caucasian Chalk Circle* is doubly reinforced through this device: peasants fighting over a valley come to accept that it should be developed along the lines best for it, just as the baby in the chalk circle is given to the mother who will care for it most.

The play about the chalk circle has dramatic episodes and **linking songs**. The Singer develops the narrative and comments on the events.

The first three acts follow the story of the servant Grusha and the trials and tribulations that befall her as a result of her saving the life of an abandoned baby boy. At the end of the third act, she is forced to go to court, as the child's aristocratic biological mother demands the boy back. The city judge who presides over her case is called Azdak, and at the beginning of Act 4, the play jumps back two years and traces the story of how he became city judge, allowing the audience to learn more about his character and the type of person he represents. In Act 5, Azdak listens to Natella and Grusha's claims for the child Michael. He then asks for the child to be placed in a chalk circle and tells the two women that the one who can pull Michael out of the circle can keep him. Twice Natella pulls on the child and Grusha lets go, unable to harm the child she has come to love. Azdak awards Michael to Grusha.

The play adheres to many of Brecht's notions about theatre, in particular the **Verfremdungseffekt**. The fact that most of the action takes place as a play within a play, with narrative and commentary, means that the audience is continually forced to recognise that they are watching theatre and to reflect on this. This is reinforced by the songs. The leaps in time also serve to distance the audience from the actual events on stage and encourage them to think about what it all means.

However, in the scene between Simon and Grusha when he returns from the war and Michael is taken by the Ironshirts, Grusha is put in a personal dilemma with which the audience cannot fail to empathise and this scene of pure drama leads to an exciting **denouement**. The scene is naturally dramatic, but what can we find in it to teach our audience?

The Caucasian Chalk Circle includes examples of Brecht's **gestic acting**. For example, notice Grusha's act of showing her hands to the elegant young lady. It is not just that Grusha's hands are cracked, showing that she is a servant (which for the elegant young lady confirms the power relationship), but it is also that the submissive, physical gesture of showing her hands in the first place tells us much about Grusha, 'the sucker', as Brecht, relishing the American slang, called her.

Brecht deliberately mixes brief sparse **poetry** and **song**, with a **formal dialogue** and **realistic slang**. The final scene in Azdak's court contains the lawyers' formal court pleading; Grusha conducting a domestic scene with Simon while at the same time shouting and fighting her corner with the judge; Simon and Azdak trading **aphorisms**; and the Singer telling us what Grusha thinks but is too angry to say, in increasingly abstract poetry.

Brecht's skill at creating tension is evident throughout *The Caucasian Chalk Circle*. For example, in Grusha's crossing of the bridge to escape the Ironshirts, the audience is told through the Singer and through Grusha's song that the bridge is rotten, that it is a risk to cross it and that attempting to do so tempts God. Certainly

Despite Brecht's (and Marxism's) hostility to organised religion, he cannot have failed to know the biblical story of the judgement of Solomon: 1 Kings 3. Soloman had to decide which of two women was the mother of a baby, so he ordered that the child, still alive, be cut into two halves, and one half given to each woman. One of the women said that she would rather give up her claim to the baby than let it be killed, so Solomon knew that she was the real mother.

Elements of the performing arts

❝ For all the yards of theory about Brechtian alienation, I am also struck by how involving the story is in human terms. ❞

Michael Billington, *Guardian* 24/08/87.

Notice that the key characters have names, while the lesser roles are referred to in a more general representative way.

it instructs the audience that human beings can do extraordinary feats in extraordinary circumstances, but they cannot fail to want to know whether she (and the child) will survive.

Similarly, while the episodic approach to her progress through the mountains is broken up into significant moments, there is the underlying tension of the constant threat of being caught out. In this, it is easy to see parallels from Brecht's own past, as until he fled Germany after the Reichstag fire, he had been number five on the Nazi hit list. He moved through Europe to America, but had to flee again later after appearing before the House Committee for Un-American Activities.

Checklist

Here is a summary of the main aspects of Brecht's theatre discussed above. You should see how these fingerprints apply to the play that you are studying.

- ☑ Brecht's **reaction against the theatre prevalent at the time** – an art form that existed as entertainment for the bourgeois classes.

- ☑ **Political and social issues** as inspiration for the plays.

- ☑ **Epic theatre** developed by Brecht – forced the audience to think actively for themselves about the issues presented. Distanced them from engaging in the action: **Verfremdungseffekt**.

- ☑ Structure – usually **episodic**, with attention deliberately drawn to structural elements.

- ☑ **Selfconscious theatricality** also demonstrated by clear **juxtapositions**, introductions to scenes, **narrator comments**, and features such as songs and poems to divide scenes.

- ☑ **Actors distanced from their characters** – presenting them rather than becoming them. Use of **gestus**. Prevents audience from becoming emotionally involved.

- ☑ **Cast** remained on stage and changed costume in view of the audience – lack of pretence of realistic theatre.

- ☑ **Mechanisms** of the theatre deliberately not hidden.

Web link

Godber's own website is very comprehensive, with biography, lists of plays and transcriptions of talks: www.johngodber.co.uk.

John Godber

Born in 1956, the son of a miner in west Yorkshire, John Godber is now reckoned to be the third most frequently performed British playwright after Shakespeare and Alan Ayckbourn – no mean feat for an ex-drama teacher and television-soap scriptwriter.

Context and influences

Teaching experience

Probably the most frequently quoted fact about John Godber is that he trained and worked as a drama teacher at the school he attended in his youth. The envy of many an ambitious drama teacher, he wrote successful plays, winning the National Student Drama Festival while still teaching. He drew on that experience for many of his characters, situations and short, crisp dialogue – especially in *Teechers* and the later *Thick as a Brick*.

Godber's experience in school performance work made him aware of the necessary economy of setting and propping, thanks to minimal space and resources, but he still emphasised high production and performance values. He proves that you don't need vast arrays of costume, flash lighting rigs or impressive auditoriums to make fine performances. As a teacher he was used to doing everything himself on a minimal budget.

While still working as a drama teacher, Godber started writing for television. *Crown Court* was a lunchtime television drama, featuring a single case over two or three episodes, with the majority of the action based in a crown court. The cases were presented as if they were real, with a very brief introduction to the case and all the characters concerned. This exploited the natural sense of performance, conflict and tension of a court, but also provided the challenge of making sure each one had sufficient human, social and dramatic interest to keep the audience interested, given the limitations of the same courtroom setting from one case to the next.

He also worked on the children's soap opera *Grange Hill*, based around life at an east London school, and *Brookside*, a domestic soap set in a suburban housing estate on the outskirts of Liverpool. Though the characters were ordinary people, they ended up living extraordinary lives, as in television drama something gripping has to be happening all the time – and by the end the plot lines had got increasingly outlandish. However, Godber drew on his television work when writing for the theatre.

In 1984, Godber took over as director of Hull Truck Theatre Company. He converted what was then a highly respected but elitist company into a local community theatre, performing plays that feature characters such as teachers, coal-board workers and waitresses. The company is now financially successful and has gone on to do West End runs, country-wide tours and television sitcoms.

When discussing Godber's technique and style, remember that you are dealing with a period of more than 20 years, during which he has been highly prolific. What could be said about *Bouncers* may not necessarily apply to *Cramp*, for example. While the more recent plays still tend to be rooted in the social and cultural background of Yorkshire, they have developed a more reflective, wistful atmosphere. Make sure you know when the play you are studying was written so that you are aware of what point in his career it is from.

Godber is unashamedly populist in his approach to theatre. His themes concern the world that ordinary people inhabit. He has talked on several occasions about the importance of accessibility to live theatre for 'ordinary folk'. Since moving to Hull, he has written plays for the people of Hull. If they have resonance elsewhere and are able to tour then he is happy for them to do so, but his loyalty is to the local community.

Regional writing has long been a feature of British theatre. Scottish theatre has always had a distinctive edge, but perhaps a more relevant parallel is the Manchester School of the early part of the 20th century. This small group of playwrights, most prominently Brighouse (*Hobson's Choice*) and Houghton (*Hindle Wakes*),

Television writing

“ I'm clear now that the reason that I stopped doing *Grange Hill* and *Brookside* was because I wasn't able to express how I felt about the world, and unless you're opening a vein with the writing there seems to be no point doing it, so it has to matter to you really emotionally. ”

Godber in Talkback at Hull Truck Theatre, 2001. Taken from interview transcript on www.johngodber.co.uk/interviews/ hulltalk.pdf.

Hull Truck Theatre

Regional and cultural influences

“ I'm from a mining background, mining's not particularly sexy, if you want to close a theatre, put on a play about mining…it's something that I try to do to broaden the canvas. ”

Godber at Derby Playhouse, 1996. www.johngodber.co.uk/interviews/ derby.pdf.

created social realism with a particular Lancashire colour and, without overdoing the 'clogs and shawls' element, created comedies from the ordinary lives of local people.

Stylistic influences

The influence of Godber's experience in writing for television is particularly evident in his theatre work. The fast pace generated by scenes cutting from one to another and the rapid exposition of only the necessary elements, laying trails for what will happen later, are characteristic of his plays. Similarly, the short episodic scenes and the rapid story-telling with multiple plot lines are used in Godber's theatre, and the message of the play is often underlined for the audience at important points.

> **Tip**
>
> Remember that these influences are identified after the event. The value of drawing conclusions about stylistic parallels is in understanding how the plays work as theatre. If your aim is to create drama in the style of Godber or perform his work as repertoire, then you need to understand where it has come from, how it has been put together, how the pieces fit, in order to breathe life into them.

Classical and renaissance theatre

There are also other, less modern stylistic influences identifiable in Godber's work, as he re-uses traditional classical forms and conventions in a postmodernist way. The use of **verse** and **choral speech** punctuating the dialogue, prologues and **epilogues**, narration, song, episodic scenes, even the idea of a comic playing a variety of roles harks back to the theatre of ancient Rome. Much of this classicism was re-used in the work of renaissance writers, especially Shakespeare whose influence on Godber can be seen in *Up 'n' Under*, for example, and in the mixture of verse and **prose**, and the fast-paced witty dialogue. Other features are reminiscent of commedia dell' arte, such as the stock characters and the simple, real situations in which the banal, the trite and the mundane are made extraordinary. Underlying the comic elements is usually a serious message to the audience.

Structure and form

This mixture of traditional and modern is especially noticeable in the structure of Godber's plays, with the episodic, fast-moving nature of television drama blended with dramatic forms such as prologues and epilogues.

A Godber play is characterised by a well-controlled and dynamic sense of pace and energy. This can be defined in terms of momentum of the performance and an impression of latent potential throughout the piece. It does not mean that everything is taken at the hectic pace of *Bouncers* or *Shakers*. The two partner pieces *Happy Jack* and *September in the Rain* have the same characteristic quality of a specific pace, but they are more mellow and, at times, still. If you try to rush or slow down the pace of a Godber play, you will lose the mood and sense.

Unities

A play which adheres to all three dramatic unities will take place in one location, over a single period of time (no flashbacks or leaps forward) and will tell a single story, relating only those events which are important to this central plot.

Godber's pieces usually have unity of time, with a specific time-span such as a holiday, three school terms or an event such as the office party. There is usually a contained location, from which we might be taken to other places but the action returns to the same place. Godber's early plays tend to lack a controlled continuity of action.

Elements of performing arts

The language in Godber's plays can be seen as a self-conscious mixture of coarse northern dialect and the poetic, much of which is designed to create comic effect. The working-class characters, around whom Godber's plays revolve, will sometimes switch from their everyday slang and swearing into a pretentious language and tone of voice. This creates humour, but also **irony**.

Godber's plays tend to mix a number of types of dialogue. Often there is a lengthy narrative speech interrupted by a single line, controlling the pace. He uses choral one-liners in many of his early plays to emphasise and punctuate the flow of the drama. Monologues are used to inform the audience and narrative is often used to set the scene.

Godber also mixes in verse and rhyme, heightening the dialogue but often creating irony, for instance when he has working class characters speak coarse language in verse. Even forms such as rap appear. *Up 'n' Under* uses verse and poetry with multiple references and **allusions** to Shakespearean and other poetic texts.

Some students think that **multi-role playing** is an invention of the later part of the 20th century, and of Godber's in particular. It isn't. Driven by economic necessity, in the same way that Shakespeare and his contemporaries were, Godber found that using a small number of actors to play a large number of parts is the cheapest way to work on a broad canvas with a range of roles. It also adds a quite different dimension to the performance for the audience, since much of the enjoyment is gained from watching the speed and dexterity of the character changes. However, it does require a very flexible performer to do justice to the range of characters and their differences.

One aspect that Godber found useful here was to have stereotypical characters. By selecting types, jobs, roles and so on that have built-in assumptions, there is already a shorthand at work. Many of these types are working class and we tend to be sympathetic towards them even when they are behaving in unpleasant ways. We are left with the sense of a not unkind caricature. Godber appears to have a somewhat contradictory or ambivalent attitude to the working class and the lower-middle class: he notes their pretensions and their limited perceptions of what life holds for them, but balances this by presenting their sense of contentment, self-worth and satisfaction in an endearing way. Often there is great irony in this ambivalence.

Godber is well known for his minimal sets. In the same way that he requires his actors to show great dexterity, and play a number of roles in basic costumes that allow them to switch rapidly, his sets also require great imagination on the part of the audience. His plays tend to be set in everyday places such as a pub, classroom or disco, with which the audience is likely to be familiar.

Godber's sharp observation of language and behaviour gives us much to laugh at, but this is balanced by what Godber called 'opening a vein' (see page 79). We are conscious of a playwright's

Language

Characterisation

Staging

Opening a vein

See pages 73–76 on Brecht's epic theatre and technique of making the audience aware of the theatre they witness.

If two things seem incongruous, they seem to be conflicting or inconsistent. We would not expect to see them together.

voice at work and this makes us consider why we are being shown what we see on stage.

This balance manifests itself in other ways. In language, there is a sudden shift from a quaint northern coarseness to sudden poetic reflection; in mood, a seesaw between angry violence and happy-go-lucky calm. In action and attitude, there is a constant shifting between clowning around and humiliation.

The audience is encouraged to enjoy the way the play is being performed through the undercutting of theatrical conventions, with minimal props, costume changes and the use of mime and choreographed actions. The audience is also often addressed directly. We describe this technique as self-conscious theatricality, because the playwright is exploiting the conventions of the medium that both they and the audience understand well. Shakespeare does this in *A Midsummer Night's Dream* and *Hamlet*, for example, and Michael Frayn employs it in *Noises Off*.

Godber creates humour through irony and particularly through exaggeration. Seeing characters discussing banal and mundane subjects on stage seems incongruous and comic.

Music and dance

Music is central to many Godber plays. Whether contemporary chart music or specific tunes detailed in the text, music is used to set the mood, period and pace of the performance. For example: *Shakers Re-stirred* uses the Housemartins' *Happy Hour*; Puccini is used throughout *Gym and Tonic*; Kitty Kallen and Mario Lanza appear in *Happy Jack*; Ken Dodd features in *September in the Rain*; *Cramp* uses a live band on stage; and *Thick as a Brick* is a musical.

Godber's work needs to be highly choreographed to achieve the right speed and effect – not only when characters are actually dancing, but also in terms of the physical movements that they perform, particularly when characters are expected to perform certain actions in unison. Since actors often play more than one role, their physicality can be crucial to establishing and maintaining character.

Bouncers

Context and influences

Further reading

Bouncers by John Godber (Josef Weinberger Plays 2000).

" Keep it alive for today. Make it work for your particular actors, in your particular space, and you will have a first-class production of *Bouncers*. "

Godber, from his author's note to *Bouncers*.

Bouncers is set in and around a nightclub called Mr Cinders. The play was first performed in 1977 at the Edinburgh Fringe Festival, but it is still as relevant today in its examination of a nightclub's clientele and staff. Godber is specific that the play should be adapted to make sure that it is relevant to its audience as times change. Only four actors perform in the play, taking the role of one of the four bouncers as well as other young men and women who visit the club. One of Godber's early plays, it displays many features that are characteristic of his work.

One of the most obvious features of *Bouncers* that makes it characteristic of Godber is its **location** in the north of England and its focus on the working classes. Even in a play that centres around a nightclub, there are references to mining that remind us of Godber's own background:

LES [*as Rosie*]   And soon my face looks like a miner's back in the showers, rivulets of black Max Factor.

Like much of Godber's work, the structure of *Bouncers* is **episodic**. The action resembles more a sequence of interlaced scenarios, held together by the main characters, making up a whole. The stereotyped characters arriving at the disco form mini scenes in themselves. The characters often provide links between episodes as they switch roles and introduce themselves as their new character. Eric introduces the play with a classical-style prologue, his speeches are signalled by the other three actors, the interval is announced by the bouncers and the action of the play is framed by the bouncers' rap.

Music and lighting are also crucial to switches of scene and role, and they emphasise the fast pace at which these happen. Godber specifies the televisual features of *Bouncers* in his author's note to the play:

> Directors of the play should never think of Chekhov; rather they should think of cartoons and cinematic techniques. The play was conceived for an audience that regards the theatre as box sets, big red curtains and tedious actors. The theatre can certainly be all that – but it can also be *Bouncers*.

All the **action** takes place in the space of one day, through the lens of one evening at Mr Cinders, with the particular focus on the four doormen. With the use of time-shifts, we also see the clubbers anticipating their night out and later reflecting on it round the hot-dog stand, but we always return to the bouncers.

Rather like the zoom feature on a camera, at times we are given the wider angle, the bigger picture. For example, in Lucky Eric's second speech he takes us to a pub at Christmas, where we are given a situation that complements the activity in the nightclub, but also provides an insight into Eric's character and potential. At other times, we are zoomed back in to details of the here and now: 'at about twelve o'clock, the toilets are the hell-hole of the disco…'.

The **language** of *Bouncers* is typical of Godber's work. The characters use coarse language, employing slang and swear words. The everyday language of working-class characters is contrasted with the upper-class rugby players who are **parodied** by the bouncers:

ALL (*chanting in an upper-class accent*) Jolly boating weather, fa la la la la…

RALPH   Supposed to be bleeding educated.

There is also a formal use of rhyme and rhythm, not only in the opening and closing 'Bouncers Rap', but also elsewhere, used to create comic effect:

ERIC   It's ten past one. Baz is well gone.

This coarse language is sometimes mixed with a more heightened, poetic vocabulary. The unexpected combination of these two apparently conflicting forms again creates comic effect. It also creates irony, adding a self-conscious element to the dialogue, because we are aware that the effect has been created deliberately:

LES   In the urinals, there is by this time a liberal smattering of tab ends and the odd soupçon of sick.

Structure and form

Further study

See what you can find out about Chekhov and consider what Godber means here when he compares his own play to Chekhov's theatre.

Elements of the performing arts

This mixture of crude and sophisticated is particularly evident in Lucky Eric's speeches. Elsewhere, much of the dialogue consists of single lines, constantly driving the play along, with frequent choral interjections that comment on the play itself.

Again typical of Godber's writing is the predominance of a number of **stereotypical characters** in *Bouncers*, played by just four actors. He often creates character from just a few stereotypical but keenly observed characteristics, all the more important when just four actors are playing a wide variety of roles. Godber's sympathy towards the working classes comes through in his portrayal of middle-class characters – such as the punter at the end of *Bouncers* looking for one more bottle of champagne or the group from St Luke's – as subjects of ridicule, less attractive to the audience. Yet, as always, his attitude is an ambivalent one and we have to remain aware of when we are laughing *with* and when *at* the working-class characters.

The stereotypes are reinforced by the characters themselves, as they introduce themselves when first switching into a role:

ERIC   Maureen. Massive but nice. Fat but cuddly. Not a bag but likes a drink and a laugh. A bit busty.

This **self-conscious theatricality** is one of Godber's fingerprints and it is prominent in *Bouncers*. There are moments when the audience is addressed directly, for example when Judd asks them 'What are you laughing at?'. They are reminded that they are watching a play as the actors comment on the play itself:

ERIC   Ralph, get the kettle on… Les, get the chocolate biscuits out…

JUDD   Why?

ERIC   It's the interval.

The chanted chorus of 'social comment' underlines for us that much of what we hear is deliberately intended to be ironic. We laugh at the antics of the girls in the disco, who appear in control, but Lucky Eric's monologue gives us a different picture. Similarly, when we hear the couple's thoughts and opinions about each other, there is comedy tinged with sympathy.

As with many of Godber's works, other art forms are important in *Bouncers*. Since it is set in a nightclub, the **music** and **lighting** are crucial to set the scene and create the necessary atmosphere of the disco. The characters sing along to the records in the disco and the popularity of this play spawned the 'Bouncers Rap' as a single.

Typically, there are few **props** – just a couple of beer kegs and four handbags are specified by Godber. The stage is bare, making the music and lighting yet more important in setting the scenes and establishing mood and atmosphere.

Of necessity in a play centred around a nightclub, we see **dance**, but it ranges from Zulu warriors and girls round a handbag, to *Shalamar*, to the drunken feeling-up of partners at the end of the evening – and even a parody of Michael Jackson's *Thriller*.

> "I've changed because those of you who might have seen my earlier plays like *Bouncers* and *Teechers* and *Shakers* and *Up 'n' Under* – they're quite physical plays, they're quite stylised plays but as I've got older I'm getting a lot more sitting down acting."
>
> Godber in Talkback at the Hull Truck Theatre.

Godber said of *Bouncers* that it is 'very in-yer-face, visceral physical theatre' and the actors who perform in it need to be very physically flexible. The choral/unison work is vitally important to the presentation even if it is uniformly zipping-up flies in a toilet. The actions that the lads use in downing and counting their pints need to be carefully controlled and precise at the start, so that by the fifth or sixth, the audience notices the effect of the drink on their coordination. The tight, uniform approach also allows the action to be undercut to create comic moments. So, in the first example above, one of the zips gets stuck, or catches on something, because the character doing the zipping is showing off.

Godber in conversation with Alan Ayckbourn and Tim Firth. 'Visceral' refers literally to the inner parts of the body or intestines, and is therefore used metaphorically to mean that something is deep-seated, emotional or profound.

Checklist

Here is a list of Godber's fingerprints: see how many of these apply to your play and in what ways.

- ☑ Godber's experiences as a **drama teacher** and in **television writing** have been hugely influential on his playwriting, from the subjects he chooses to write about to the structure of the plays and the sets he specifies.
- ☑ Structure – usually made up from **many short episodes** that move at a **fast pace**.
- ☑ Characters are **stereotypes**, mainly **working class** and often from the north of England, and a small number of actors multi-role many parts.
- ☑ **Humour** and **irony** are used to convey **serious social and political messages**.
- ☑ The theatricality of the plays is **self-conscious** and the audience is often directly addressed.
- ☑ **Sets are minimal** and there are **few props**.
- ☑ **Music** and **dance** feature prominently in Godber's plays, helping to create atmosphere as well as aiding the structure by dividing or linking scenes.

George Gershwin

George Gershwin (1898–1937) was one of the most successful writers of American popular song in the 20th century, although strangely the shows from which many of these songs were taken were flops and enjoyed only short runs on Broadway. Gershwin mainly wrote songs, but be careful of categorising him simply as a songwriter, since he also wrote a few orchestral pieces and an opera (*Porgy and Bess*). It was his dream to be respected as an orchestral composer; he is most often thought of as a songwriter, however.

Categorising Gershwin can also be difficult in the sense that he seems to defy the traditional distinction between classical and popular music, combining both jazz and classical styles. As you are studying only the songs, though, you should be able to understand Gershwin's compositional techniques without getting bogged down in this debate.

There is a strong tradition of 20th-century American composers from Jewish backgrounds. These include Aaron Copland, Leonard Bernstein and Steve Reich. Some attempts have been made to show that George Gershwin's song melodies were influenced by the sound of Jewish synagogue music.

Gershwin became friends with composers Maurice Ravel and Arnold Schoenberg, and hoped that they would give him formal training in composition. Both refused. Schoenberg memorably suggested that to do so would turn Gershwin into a second-rate Schoenberg rather than a first-rate Gershwin!

Tin Pan Alley

Context and influences

Gershwin's parents, of Russian-Jewish descent, were first-generation immigrants to America. They were keen to integrate into American culture and create a new identity for themselves, changing their name from Gershovitz to Gershwin.

There was no history of music in the Gershwin family and this lack of musical background was a source of concern for George Gershwin. While commercially he was a highly successful composer, it is clear that throughout his career he yearned for formal training in the techniques of harmony, **counterpoint** and **orchestration**.

His first teacher was Charles Hambitzer (d.1918) who introduced Gershwin to the classical piano **repertoire**, particularly the 19th-century composers Frederick Chopin (1810–1849) and Franz Liszt (1811–1886). In the 1920s, Gershwin was taught by the experimental composer Henry Cowell (1897–1965), although none of Cowell's radical ideas about music found their way into Gershwin's compositions.

It is hard now to imagine a world without readily available recorded music. At the turn of the 20th century, however, the vast majority of music was performed live from music notation. Early phonograph recordings were certainly available but they were not the main method of selling popular music. Music was generally notated and this is a major difference between the production of popular music at the start of the 21st century and that written 100 years ago. If you buy the sheet music to a song by a contemporary artist, it is likely to have been **transcribed** from a recorded performance. However, at the start of the 20th century, the reverse process took place: the sheet music was used by performers as the basis of the recording.

One area of New York, from 29th Street, between Broadway and 6th Avenue, achieved fame for promoting songs through the sale of sheet music. This was the main leisure and entertainment area of the city and was ideally placed for people looking to buy the sheet music from shows they'd been to. Music publishing was big business during the early part of the 20th century and songs were printed and sold in large volume. Each publisher employed songwriters and 'song pluggers', though one person could perform both these roles. The song pluggers, as the name suggests, were salesmen who played the songs to people interested in buying them. The song plugger, usually a man, would have a parlour where he would play songs for any potential buyer. The plugger had to be a skilled musician, able to **transpose** the song into a higher or lower key if a customer needed it. The noise of so many song pluggers in such a small geographical area made a clattering, jangling sound which was reminiscent of a large number of pots and pans being rattled together. This is how the area became known as 'Tin Pan Alley'.

No matter how good the song plugger, though, it was the songwriter's skills that were the most important. Tin Pan Alley songs were written to a simple and well-established formula, and it was up to the songwriter to be as creative and inventive as possible. At the age of 15, Gershwin began work for Jerome H. Remick and Company, one of the most important music publishers in Tin Pan Alley. As a songwriter and song plugger he would have gained extensive experience and knowledge regarding the best ways to create catchy melodies, interesting songs and effective arrangements. While hardly any of his Tin Pan Alley songs survive, he was later able to build on this experience to create popular music that has stood the test of time.

Gershwin's approach as a songwriter was way beyond anything that Tin Pan Alley composers produced. His gift of melodic invention, his ear for interesting harmony and his ability to craft an original song – not to mention his abilities as a pianist and performer – meant that by 1917, at the age of 19, he decided to leave Remick's in search of a career that led very soon to Broadway and ultimately to Hollywood.

Form and structure

Gershwin's experience of working in Tin Pan Alley gave him a keen awareness of how to write songs to a formula. Those songwriters churned out songs one after another, many of them to the same pattern. The verse was often less memorable than the chorus and the trick was to write a chorus with a melody that would stay in people's minds so they would continue to hum it after only a few hearings.

The formula used by many of the writers on Tin Pan Alley was not written down but it became established as many songwriters used it. The song generally opens with a short instrumental section, usually played by the piano. The verse is then used to set the scene for the song in terms of its subject matter, which is often fairly restricted in scope – exaltation, love, longing and rejection – so that it could be captured in a few words. Over time, the verse became less important and was at times even omitted completely in performance because of the performer's desire to get to the chorus, which was more well known.

The chorus was usually a 32-bar melody divided into four phrases of eight bars each. The pattern of the overall melody was AABA, which means that phrases 1, 2 and 4 were more or less the same (and so referred to as A). The third phrase (B) provided a contrast and was often termed the 'release' section of the melody. Here the key of the melody might change, or a new section of melody might be used to change the mood of the song or reflect the meaning of the words. The chorus might be repeated in its entirety or there might be another verse before the chorus returned.

Gershwin was not a great innovator in terms of form. Many of his songs, particularly the early ones, are a variation on this standard pattern and he was content to take a conventional form and work within it. The challenge was to be as original as possible within the confines of such a form rather than try to invent a totally new form. You will find, though, that some of his later songs adapt this pattern: you need to be clear what the structure is of each of the four songs that you study.

Tip

Don't spend your time in the exam writing a narrative history of Tin Pan Alley – the examiners know it already. However, do make sure you understand how Gershwin was influenced by the style of those songwriters.

Elements of the performing arts

One important aspect of Gershwin's songs that you need to be aware of is that George Gershwin wrote the music *before* his brother Ira Gershwin wrote the lyrics. This may not seem particularly radical, but it was accepted practice in classical music that a composer would take existing words and set them to music. The meaning of the words would inspire the composer to produce a melody that would reflect the mood of these words. George Gershwin, though, was convinced of the greatness of his melodies and was happy for his brother Ira to produce words – often painstakingly – that would fit these melodies. If you find examples of **word painting**, therefore, you need to remember that this was not primarily thanks to George's ability as a composer but rather Ira's skill as a lyricist. You also need to be aware that although Ira was his main lyricist, George Gershwin also wrote songs with other people, such as DuBose Heyward (who wrote the words for *Summertime*).

Ira Gershwin's lyrics are generally witty and have a strong sense of rhythm to match that of the music. There are many examples of clever rhyming schemes and lines that flow very naturally. These lines from the 1937 song *Nice Work if you can Get It* are an excellent example of Ira's rhyming schemes:

> The man who only lives for making money
> Lives a life that isn't necessarily sunny.
> Likewise the man who works for fame,
> There's no guarantee that time won't erase his name.
> The fact is, the only work that really brings enjoyment
> Is the kind that is for girl and boy meant,
> Fall in love you won't regret it,
> That's the best work of all if you can get it.

You might notice that occasionally he has changed the natural order of the words to create a rhyme. This is sometimes referred to as a forced rhyme. There are several examples of this type of forced rhyme in other Gershwin songs and they almost certainly result from trying to fit words to music that was already composed. In some cases, not only are the rhymes forced, but the words also make little sense. The 1928 song *How Long has this been Going On?* has a highly memorable chorus which perfectly fits the mood and shape of the melody, but the verses that precede this chorus seem almost embarrassing by comparison. The first verse opens with these lyrics:

> As a tot, when I trotted in little velvet panties,
> I was kissed by my sisters, my cousins and my aunties.
> Sad to tell, it was Hell, an inferno worse than Dante's.
> So, my dear, I swore, "Never, never more".

Each line of this verse rhymes its third syllable with its sixth ('tot', 'trot' etc.), though in the last line that internal rhyme is shifted to an assonance or half rhyme between third and fifth syllables ('dear', 'swore') which is overwhelmed by the rhyme between fifth and final syllables ('swore', 'more').

As the name implies, blue notes are related to the style of singing called the blues. In this style of singing, it was customary for African-American singers to change some notes of the musical

Lyrics

The two men worked in very different ways: George was a workaholic who produced music effortlessly; Ira was a relaxed man who would spend a considerable amount of time refining a set of words to fit George's music.

Ira Gershwin was inspired by lyrics from the 19th-century English operettas of Gilbert and Sullivan. The style of the songs in these operettas was often witty and satirical with clever rhymes and jaunty melodies. He became a friend of W. S. Gilbert and aspired to imitate the English writer's style.

If you write about the relationship of the words and music in the exam, remember to keep your answer focused on the links between these two aspects. You need to show that you have a good understanding of the musical elements as well as the lyrical elements: if you put too much emphasis on just discussing the words, you may lose marks.

Ira Gershwin used this technique on many occasions. In *They all laughed at Christopher Columbus*, Ira uses an internal rhyme scheme on the line 'they told Marconi wireless was a phoney' and in *It ain't necessarily so* (from the opera *Porgy and Bess*) there is an internal rhyme in the line 'de things dat yo' li'ble to read in de Bible'.

Blue notes

scale to produce a sad or even heart-rending effect. The third and the seventh notes of the **major scale** tend to be altered to produce this effect. If you take a scale of C (from any C on the piano keyboard to the next C) there are seven notes. If the first note is C, then the second is D, the third is E and so on. You can see this in the example in the margin.

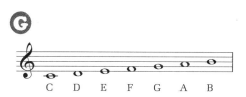

Now experiment with changing the third note to E♭ rather than E or the seventh note to B♭ rather than B and see what effect it has on a melody. Although you will not need to explain this in the exam, if you make appropriate references to it then the examiners will know that you are talking about.

One example of blue notes in Gershwin's melodies is from *I'll Build a Stairway to Paradise*, written in 1922 and therefore one of his earliest hits after leaving Tin Pan Alley. This melody seems to be based on a line from a 12-bar blues – listen particularly to the notes on the words 'Paradise', 'day' and 'any'. These are blue notes based on the seventh note of the chord in each case.

Gershwin did not invent the use of the blue note. There are plenty of examples of other music that used them, mainly popular music such as folk and jazz. They can also be found in traditional Jewish music although there is no evidence that Gershwin was especially influenced by this.

Blue seventh notes are also used as a focus point for the end of each bar of music in the 1924 song, *The Man I Love*. Listen to the words 'along', 'love' and 'strong'. This succession of blue sevenths makes the music sound as if the singer is yearning to meet the imaginary man she is singing about.

There are also many examples of Gershwin using blue notes on the third note of the scale rather than the seventh. In the first phrase of the 1924 song *Somebody Loves Me*, the melody keeps switching between the expected third note and the flattened or blue third note. On the phrase 'I wonder who' the first two notes are the ones you would expect in the scale (the white note B) but the word 'who' is set to a 'blue' note, the note B♭ in this case.

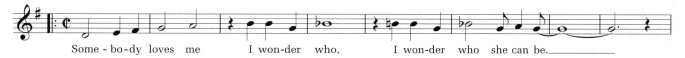

Chromatic melodies

The word chromatic literally means 'colourful', but in the context of music it refers to notes that do not occur in a particular scale or key. So if a piece of music is 'in C', all notes not in the scale of C are unexpected splashes of colour. In that sense, chromatic notes are similar to blue notes but they are not restricted to the third or the seventh notes of the scale. When they are used sensitively, they can give a very soulful, yearning feel to a melody and George

Since Gershwin was only 39 when he died in 1937, 'later' refers to the songs he wrote in the mid-1930s.

Gershwin made significant use of them in his later songs. Look at the opening of the 1937 song *They Can't Take that Away from Me*. The fourth word 'won't' introduces a chromatic note and the second phrase 'though by tomorrow you're gone' has two further chromatic notes, F♯ and G♯. This sets the mood for the rest of the melody.

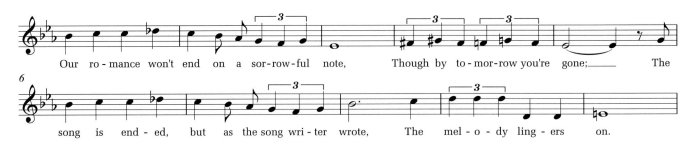

The use of **chromatic notes** is even more noticeable in 'It Ain't Necessarily So', taken from his 1935 opera *Porgy and Bess*. In the opening phrase, Gershwin uses two chromatic notes, D♭ and C♭, which create some uncertainty as to where the melody is going. This is picked up in Ira's lyrics 'it ain't necessarily so'.

Pentatonic melodies

In a pentatonic tune there are only five different notes. If you play all the black notes on the piano, you will hear what one pentatonic scale sounds like. Some musicians – often self-taught ones – have relied on the technique of playing on the black notes. The songwriter Irving Berlin (1888–1989), for example, would play all of his songs in F♯ major. The pentatonic scale uses the first, second, third, fifth and sixth notes of the scale. In the key of G, these notes would be as shown in the margin.

Gershwin composed a number of melodies that make use of the pentatonic scale. While these melodies are not completely pentatonic, there is enough usage for it to be obvious.

The first three lines of the 1937 song *Nice Work if you can Get It* are pentatonic as you can see by comparing the notes in this melody with the notes in the margin above.

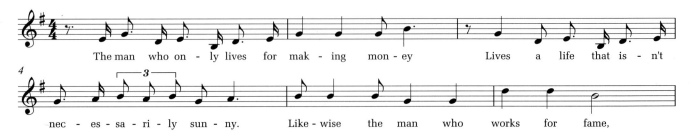

To take another example, one of Gershwin's most famous songs *I Got Rhythm* (written in 1930) is pentatonic except for the chromatic note on the word 'who'.

Discussing Gershwin's songs

You will be expected to have studied **four** contrasting songs by George Gershwin. Your teacher will choose the songs that you should study and they do **not** need to be the same as the ones we have chosen. We have chosen three songs that show a range of Gershwin's techniques and offer some contrasts. You will need to apply the same techniques to the study of at least one other song and make sure that you know each of the songs in the same amount of detail. They are discussed here in the order in which they were written.

Swanee

Swanee (1919) was Gershwin's first major hit and was written two years after he left Tin Pan Alley. It gives us the first glimpse into the style that he developed after his years of working as a song plugger.

The words are not by Ira Gershwin – it was not until the mid-1920s that Ira became fully established as George's libretticist. The whole song takes its inspiration from a very well known song by the 19th-century American songwriter Stephen C. Foster, *Swanee River* (sometimes referred to as 'The Old Folks at Home'). Foster's nostalgic lyrics form the basis of the lyrics of *Swanee*.

The song was used in a live revue at the Capitol Theatre, New York and received the razzamatazz associated with the Ziegfeld Follies. Following the revue, the song was taken up by the popular singer Al Jolson. Jolson (who was white) sang it with his face made up in imitation of (or parody of) an African-American face. The make-up was one element in his show that was in the style of a minstrel song, a style that similarly imitated or parodied what white Americans thought black American musical entertainers sounded like. The song has references to 'mammy' and this would have helped *Swanee to* fit in Jolson's show which contained a famous a song called *Mammy*.

> **Further study**
>
> The Ziegfeld Follies were a series of spectacular song and dance and entertainment shows that were started in 1907 by the producer Florenz Ziegfeld and continued intermittently into the 1930s and slightly beyond. See what else you can find out about them and try to watch a film showing excerpts.

The form of the song is as follows:

Introduction. Four bars: F minor. This is played by the piano only.

Verse. 32 bars: F minor. This consists of lines of lyrics. Each line of music has its own musical phrase:

> I've been away from you a long time – I never thought I'd miss you so **(A)**
>
> Somehow I feel your love was real, near you I long to be **(B)**
>
> The birds are singing, it is song time – the banjos strummin' soft and low **(A)**

I know that you yearn for me too; Swanee, you're calling me. **(B)**

Chorus (sung twice). 32 bars (64 bars including repeats): F major.

> Swanee how I love you, how I love you my dear old Swanee; **(A)**
> I'd give the world to be among the folks in D I X I Even now my **(B)**
> Mammy's waiting for me, praying for me down by the Swanee, **(A)**
> The folks up north will see me no more when I go to the Swanee shore. **(B)**

Trio. 16 bars: F major. In this section both lines have the same melody.

> Swanee, Swanee, I am coming back to Swanee
> Mammy, Mammy, I love the old folks at home.

Chorus: final reprise. 32 bars: F major. You will see that the whole song is built from regular units and fits a neat pattern. In this sense it builds on Gershwin's experience of Tin Pan Alley. You can easily see the influence of the 32-bar form of song that was widely used by these songwriters. The verse breaks down the 32 bars into the form ABAB so that the second half of the melody restates the first half with hardly any differences. This is effectively binary form.

The chorus takes a similar approach and also uses the form ABAB. The trio comes between the second and third appearances of the chorus and acts as an interlude before the final appearance of the chorus. The final reprise of the chorus is the same as before and brings the song to a conclusion.

The following table shows how *Swanee* displays certain aspects of Gershwin's general style.

> Dixie (the correct spelling) was a nickname for the 'Old South', those states which had an economy based on black slaves and which had tried to break away from the USA in the civil war.

Form	The structure of the verse and chorus is regular, both being based on 32-bar structures. The introduction and trio are also regular.
	There is a contrast between the verse and chorus in the change of key. The verse is in a more reflective and melancholy key, F minor. The chorus moves to the more joyful F major.
Melody	To some extent, the melody is inspired by the character of Stephen C. Foster's melody. Like Foster's, Gershwin's melody is pentatonic and makes extensive use of the first three notes of the scale of F major.
Harmony	The harmony has some elements of jazz-inspired chords but these are not developed and the style is more akin to Dixieland. The most significant feature is the change from F minor in the verse to F major in the chorus.

Fascinating Rhythm

> Note that the title contains the word *Fascinating* rather than *Fascinatin'* as it is sometimes wrongly referred to.

Fascinating Rhythm was written in 1924 for the show *Lady Be Good!* and is one of the earliest collaborations between George and Ira Gershwin. The song reflects the structures used by the Tin Pan Alley songwriters, although Gershwin's melodies are much more complex. The song is in E♭ major and the form is as follows:

Introduction. Four bars. This is played by the piano only and is based on the opening motif of the chorus.

Verse. 16 bars. This is a regular verse of four lines, each broadly the same length. Each phrase is four bars long and the structure of this melody is based on the pattern AABB (binary form).

> Got a little rhythm, a rhythm, a rhythm that pit-a-pats through my brain, **(A)**
>
> So darn persistent, the day isn't distant when it'll drive me insane. **(A)**

Comes in the morning without any warning and hangs around all day **(B)**

I'll have to sneak up to it, someday and speak up to it, I hope it listens when I say. **(B)**

Chorus (sung twice). 32 bars (64 bars including repeats). This is a regular melody to which Ira Gershwin has composed an eight-line **stanza**. The lines are slightly longer than those in the verse and they are grouped in pairs in the chorus so that each phrase of music is eight bars long and covers two lines of lyrics. The overall form of the melody follows the pattern ABAB.

Fascinating rhythm, you've got me on the go! Fascinating rhythm, I'm all in a quiver.
What a mess you're making! The neighbours want to know why I'm always shaking just like a fivver. **(A)**

Each morning I get up with the sun, (Start a hopping never stopping)
To find at night no work has been done. I know that **(B)**

Once it didn't matter, but now you're doing wrong; when you start to patter, I'm so unhappy.
Won't you take a day off? Decide to run along somewhere far away off, and make it snappy! **(A)**

Oh how I long to be the man I used to be!
Fascinating rhythm, Oh won't you stop picking on me! **(B)**

Verse 2. This follows the same pattern as verse 1 but with different words. The song is **strophic**.

Chorus. The chorus is then sung again, and repeated, as before.

The table below discusses some of Gershwin's 'fingerprints' in *Fascinating Rhythm*.

Form	This song comes fairly early in Gershwin's mature output. Although it was produced at the same time as his piano concerto *Rhapsody in Blue*, the composer was still only 26. The influences of Tin Pan Alley are obvious and Gershwin uses the formulas AABB and ABAB for his melodies. However, he creates contrast by making the musical phrases in the chorus twice as long as in the verse.
Words	This song is an excellent example of how the words and music of the Gershwins fit together as if they were completely intended for one another. The words of the first verse introduce the idea of being haunted by a repetitive rhythm and the melody contains several repetitions of the first motif on the words 'Got a little rhythm, a rhythm, a rhythm'. The words of the chorus capture the contrasting mood – a rhythm that is genuinely 'fascinating' in the way it is syncopated and goes round the same ideas again and again in a haunting manner. The words and music seem to shift the beat in phrase A but there is a more regular rhythm on phrase B.
Harmony	The piano chords (played by the left hand) are completely regular and provide a steady beat throughout the song. This contrasts with the syncopated melody in the right hand of the piano (doubled by the voice).

They all laughed

This song was written for the 1937 show *Shall We Dance* and is an excellent example of Gershwin's mature songwriting style. Some aspects of the song are similar to his early style, while others are clearly more advanced. For example, the tune is fairly simple and makes use of pentatonic motifs. The harmony, however, shows some jazz influences and makes use of a number of chromatic chords.

The whole song is in the key of G major and the form of the song is as follows:

Introduction. Four bars. This is played by the piano only and is based on the opening melody of the chorus. It gives a short glimpse of what is to come.

Verse. 20 bars. This is less regular than some of Gershwin's verses and consists of six lines. The length of each line is irregular and the pattern of the melody is not rigid. Lines 1 and 2 are similar and lines 4 and 5 have some resemblance.

> The odds were a hundred to one against me.
> The world thought the heights were too high to climb
> But people from Missouri never incensed me.
> Oh, I wasn't a bit concerned
> For from history I had learned
> How many, many times the worm had turned.

Chorus (sung twice, with different words for repeat). 32 bars (64 bars including repeats). This is a regular melody to which Ira Gershwin has composed a regular four-line stanza. The lines are considerably longer than in the verse but the length of the lines is well balanced and the melody follows the pattern AABA.

> They all laughed at Christopher Columbus when he said the world was round, they all laughed when Edison invented sound **(A)**
>
> They all laughed at Wilbur and his brother, when they said that man could fly, they told Marconi, wireless was a phoney, it's the same old cry **(A)**
>
> They laughed at me wanting you, said I was reaching for the moon; but oh you came through, now they'll have to change their tune **(B)**
>
> They all said we never could be happy, they laughed at us and how! But ho, ho, ho! Who's got the last laugh now? **(A)**

The repeat of the chorus has different words but they have the same melody.

Ⓖ **Coda**. Four bars.

> He, he, he! Let's at the past laugh,
> Ha, ha, ha! Who's got the last laugh now?

The table below discusses some of Gershwin's 'fingerprints' in *They All Laughed*.

Form	The structure of the verse is irregular and there is a sense that the words are being made to fit an irregular melody. They do not 'scan' entirely comfortably and the lines differ considerably in length.
	The structure of the chorus is a standard 32-bar melody, derived in shape from the formula used extensively in Tin Pan Alley. The length of the lines, however, is noticeably longer and each of the 8-bar lines can be divided into two shorter phrases.
Melody	There is no use of blue notes in the melody of either verse or chorus and the whole song has an upbeat, 'laughing' tone which is captured in the words. The whole of phrase A in the chorus is pentatonic and is an excellent example of Gershwin's usage of this device.
Harmony	The harmony of the song is fairly complex and shows some influence of jazz styles. You do not need to be able to write out specific examples of this, but you could refer to the chords in the verse, perhaps quoting the bass line. Or you could make reference to the chromatic chords in the piano part between the first two phrases of the chorus. By contrast, the first four chords of the chorus consist of a pattern used extensively on Tin Pan Alley (G – E minor – A minor – D).

Checklist

Finally, here's a checklist of the musical aspects of Gershwin's songs to help you test yourself on the songs you have studied. Be prepared to compare and contrast how Gershwin handles these aspects in the four songs. Also – don't be afraid to add to this list if there's anything else that you've spotted as you've been studying the songs.

- ☑ **Tempo** – the speed of the song. Look at how it helps to establish the mood and atmosphere of the song/character.
- ☑ **Rhythm** – refer to relationship between the natural stresses of words and the rhythm of the melody – but bear in mind that the melody was written first!
- ☑ The way that the written **rhythms can be adapted in performance**, as in jazz style. Many performers use **rubato** in slower songs.
- ☑ **Harmony** – the chord construction that underpins the melody. Chord changes underneath the melody can often change the mood or atmosphere.
- ☑ **Dynamics** – examine how the changing dynamics in the song can contribute to the mood or atmosphere.
- ☑ **Relationship between the vocal melody and the accompaniment**. Look at the different styles of piano and/or instrumental writing and see how closely they reflect or differ from the vocal part.
- ☑ **Approaches to instrumental writing** – look at how the instrumentation is used to enhance the rhythmic qualities of the song (for example, the use of sustained chords to enhance longer rhythmic values in comparison with **staccato** notes for a short, abrupt effect).

Tip

Don't forget that you need to study **four** songs. We have given you three as a model to work from.

Steve Reich

It is sometimes difficult upon first hearing the music of American composer Steve Reich (b. 1936) to understand why it is so radical. It does not conform to the usual stereotypes of 20th-century art music being harsh and aggressive. The individual sounds used by Reich are unlikely to be challenging to listeners approaching his music for the first time. The most challenging and obvious feature of his music is the repetition of ideas. Reich exploited sounds in quite a different way from earlier 20th-century composers and the techniques of **serialism**. He was one of a handful of composers who was involved in the development of a style known as minimalism. His minimalist pieces are generally agreed to be those he wrote before 1976, the year in which he composed *Music for 18 Musicians*. After the mid 1970s, his work became broader and less minimalist.

Stylistic context

Minimalism refers to a style used by composers such as La Monte Young (b. 1935), Terry Riley (b. 1935), Philip Glass (b. 1937) and Reich. It is generally taken to refer to compositions produced during a short period from about 1964 to 1976. Minimalist composers were keen to strip music down to its basic elements, creating it from very limited musical material. Features that were common to minimalist compositions of this period were simple

Web link

You can find out more about Reich's music by visiting his website at www.stevereich.com.

Minimalism

'Systems music' was also a common term for minimalist compositions in the 1960s. 'Minimalism' is a term that is thought to have been first used in the 1970s by the British music critic and composer Michael Nyman (b.1944).

Further reading

You can find the essay 'Music as a Gradual Process' in *Writings on Music: 1965–2000* by Reich (Oxford University Press 2002).

> "I am interested in perceptible processes. I want to be able to hear the process happening throughout the sounding music. To facilitate closely detailed listening a musical process should happen extremely gradually."
>
> Steve Reich, 'Music as a Gradual Process' (from *Writings on Music: 1965–2000*).

Phasing

Tip

If you are asked a question about phasing in the examination, you will need to think carefully as there is no phasing in any of Reich's pieces after 1973. Instead, there is extensive use of counterpoint, and you'll need to be able to make two points: firstly, you need to observe that phasing is a very precise type of counterpoint and secondly, you will need to give some examples of counterpoint in the piece you have studied.

repetitive rhythms, **diatonic** melodies and unmoving or slowly changing harmony. Minimalist music is sometimes described as meditative and simplistic, although the compositional processes involved were often far from simple.

Reich summarised his 'minimalist' approach to composition in an essay written in 1968 called 'Music as a Gradual Process'. Reich himself never actually uses the term minimalist, but it is easy to see why the word is used to refer to his music from the 1960s, as it employs very few musical resources, which are not changed much during the course of each composition.

Reich's music has evolved gradually over the last 40 years and there have been numerous influences on his composition during this time.

Stylistic influences

Reich claimed he was a late starter to composition, since he was 14 years old before he had heard much music by other composers. At that age, however, he encountered three apparently different types of music that he claims changed the way in which he thought about music. These were: **baroque** music, initially that of J. S. Bach; bebop jazz, a style of jazz from the 1940s in which the music featured complex **chord sequences** often played at a fast speed; and the music of the composer Igor Stravinsky (1882–1971). Reich pointed out three features he thought were common to all of these different styles: extensive use of counterpoint, strong rhythms and clear **tonal** centres.

In 1964 Reich heard a Pentecostal preacher, Brother Walter, preaching in San Francisco and made tape recordings of him to use in a composition. He was impressed by the musical, sing-song way in which Brother Walter delivered his sermon and took the single phrase 'it's gonna rain' as the basis for a tape composition, *It's Gonna Rain*. Reich produced a second tape composition called *Come Out* (1965), this time using a short phrase from a teenager who had been wrongly imprisoned by the police for murder.

In both pieces, Reich used a technique called phasing. He made two identical tape loops but when he played them simultaneously on two separate tape recorders he noticed that that the two machines played at very slightly different speeds. This meant that, slowly and subtly, the two tapes got out of phase with one another and then eventually came back into synch with each other. Reich was therefore able to use the time it took for the tape loop to work through the phasing process in order to determine the length of sections and ultimately the whole of the piece.

Although Reich had discovered the principle of phasing by accident, he was determined to develop it further. In *Piano Phase* (1967) and *Violin Phase* (1967), he adapted the mechanical phenomenon for live performers. A short idea is played by one part and then another part (or parts) moves gradually out of phase and then back into phase. These pieces are written for only one instrument and the music is therefore **monotimbral**. Although it was difficult for 'live' performers to move in and out of phase, Reich was able to perfect the technique with his ensemble.

Reich wanted to explore other approaches to composition and his music in the 1970s developed in a number of ways. He started to write longer pieces, he began to write for larger instrumental combinations and he moved away from phasing.

As a student, Reich had been influenced by a number of other types of music from around the world and the 1970s were a time when he began to incorporate structures inspired by music from other cultures into his compositions. He was interested in the improvisatory nature of non-western music, which puts a greater responsibility on the performers to interact with one another while they perform. These other musics also had a different social status from traditional western music, since they do not create the same barriers between the performers and the audience. There were three specific types of music that Reich explored during the decade: west African drumming, Indonesian gamelan and Hebrew cantillation.

West African drumming. Reich spent some time with the Ewe people in Ghana in 1970. The dominance of the percussion of the African drummers appealed most to Reich, who had been trained as a percussionist in his teens and always had a love of mallet instruments. The way in which the strong beats of the various parts in the ensemble did not coincide also, naturally, was something he liked. The influence of this music can be heard most clearly in *Drumming* (1971).

Indonesian gamelan. Reich did not actually visit Indonesia, but was nevertheless inspired by the music of the gamelan and the use in gamelan music of cyclical and repetitive forms. The influence of this music can be heard most clearly in *Music for Mallet Instruments, Voices and Organ* (1973).

Hebrew cantillation. Reich was Jewish by birth but had very little contact with the Jewish faith until his mid-30s. He began learning Hebrew in order to understand the original language of the Jewish scriptures and noticed that the words each contained musical markings as to how they should be chanted, a principle known as cantillation. The influence of this music is fairly restricted but can be seen in Reich's *Octet* (1979).

Elements of the performing arts

When talking about Reich's music, it is often useful to divide it into his minimalist compositions (those between 1964 and 1976) and the compositions that came afterwards.

Reich's minimalist pieces tend to have the following features:

➤ A constant, fast tempo

➤ Short repeated motifs of either speech or melody

➤ The use of phasing (where one or more parts moves out of synch and then moves back in again over time)

➤ Monotimbral sound (all the parts are sounded by the same timbre)

➤ All the parts play all of the time

World music

Despite writing for larger instrumental combinations, most of the pieces were still performed by his own ensemble, Steve Reich and Musicians.

Further reading

Reich's interest grew from reading *Studies in African Music* by A. M. Jones (Oxford University Press 1959).

A gamelan is a percussion ensemble that includes xylophones, gongs, cymbals and drums. Many western composers in the 20th century have been influenced by the gamelan.

In the 1970s, Reich began to move away from phasing and began to experiment with building up motifs by replacing rests with notes, as in *Drumming*.

> Written for small ensemble, generally performed by the composer's own ensemble, Steve Reich and Musicians.

After the mid-1970s, Reich's compositions became less limited and therefore harder to define, so you may find that not all of these features appear in each work:

> Fast tempo, although since *Tehillim* (1981) Reich has also used occasional slower movements

> Interest in developing a range of instrumental sounds so that the pieces are polytimbral (for a range of sounds) rather than monotimbral

> Larger ensemble: several pieces in the 1980s were written for full orchestra (*Tehillim*, *The Desert Music*, *The Four Sections*, *Three Movements*)

> Renewed interest in human speech, sampled and used as the basis for compositions (*Different Trains*, *City Life*, *The Cave*, *Three Tales*)

> Interest in working with images to produce a new kind of video opera

> Interest in incorporating social commentary and/or autobiographical elements.

Reich's wife, Beryl Korot, collaborated with him on *The Cave* (1991) and *Three Tales* (1998–2002).

'All music is ethnic music'.

According to Reich, 'all music is ethnic music', by which he meant that all music is related to the time and place in which it was composed. This is the main reason that he (and other so-called minimalist composers) rejected the type of music being written in Europe in the 1960s as they felt it had little to say to contemporary Americans. One way in which Reich in particular attempted to locate his music in American culture was through the use of speech extracts of American speakers in his tape pieces of the 1960s. He did not use this technique in his works of the 1970s, but returned to it in his composition of *Different Trains* in 1988.

Different Trains

Different Trains for string quartet and pre-recorded sounds is a good example of how Reich's music in the 1980s had developed from his earlier works. Composed in 1988, it was written specifically for the Kronos Quartet, a string quartet which specialises in performing the work of contemporary composers. The recording of the piece made by the Kronos Quartet won a Grammy Award for Best Contemporary Composition in 1990.

Context

" I travelled back and forth between New York and Los Angeles from 1939 to 1942... I now look back and think that, if I had been in Europe during this period, as a Jew I would have had to ride very different trains. "

Steve Reich, *Writings on Music: 1965–2000*.

Since *Different Trains* is autobiographical, you need to know a little about Reich's life. Reich spent much of his childhood travelling between Los Angeles and New York to visit each of his divorced parents. Accompanied by his governess, Virginia, the young Reich found these journeys long and fairly uneventful. However, looking back on this experience as an adult, Reich started to make comparisons between his journeys and the journeys being made at the time (around 1939) by European Jews on their way to the gas chambers in the Second World War (1939–1945). The title of the piece reflects the very 'different trains' with very different purposes and destinations that he and they had been travelling on.

Speech recordings from five people form the basis of the piece. He also used sound effects associated with train journeys. Rather than using tape, as he had in the 1960s, however, he took advantage of the recently invented Casio FZ-1 and the Casio FZ-10M sampling keyboards, which gave him more flexibility than working with tape loops. The **pitch** of the speech sample can be changed easily on the sampling keyboard.

Reich decided that he wanted all of the music played by the string quartet to be generated by the speech samples. The way in which someone speaks is a little like singing. Everyone's voice goes up and down on certain words and this means that no two people sound identical. Once Reich had gathered his recordings, he transcribed them into musical notation. Once he had done this, the speech extracts could be used as individual motifs within his composition. Obviously, when people speak, they do not speak in a regular rhythm or exact pitch so Reich had to listen to the samples over and over again to make sure that the notation was as near as possible to the way in which the actual words were spoken.

One of the hardest things for a composer to do is to set words to music in a song or an opera. Reich avoids this conundrum as he adopts the reverse process; he makes music out of words by using speech extracts as the basis. That way, the music complements the natural rhythms and pitches of the spoken words.

Throughout *Different Trains*, the string parts imitate the melodic and rhythmic inflections of the speech extracts. Reich uses speech as a basis for creating melody and these melodies are used contrapuntally as the parts intertwine. This helps to create the effect of conversation between the speech parts. Listen out for examples of this in the piece.

The speech extracts are not played live in performance, but are on a pre-recorded tape. Also on the tape are another three layers of string quartet sounds and various train sounds. The string quartet plays along live with the recorded tape.

The piece is in three movements:

America – before the war (8 minutes 58 seconds). This movement is inspired by Reich's childhood journeys and is based on speech samples from two people Reich knew as a child: Virginia, his governess, who accompanied him on the train, and Mr Davis, the Pullman porter on the trains between New York and Los Angeles.

Europe – during the war (7 minutes 30 seconds). This movement focuses on the 'different trains' being taken by Jews who were condemned by Adolf Hitler to death in the gas chambers. It is based on speech samples from three survivors of the Holocaust: Rachella, Paul and Rachel, each of them a similar age to Reich himself.

After the war (10 minutes 30 seconds). This movement brings together the voices from the previous two movements and shows that once the war is over the 'different trains' are brought together.

Compositional process

Reich does not alter the speech samples – it's not the same as acid-house or other popular approaches in which the samples are manipulated.

'Contrapuntal' is the adjective for 'counterpoint'. See Glossary.

Form and structure

Elements of the performing arts

The score of *Different Trains* is published by Hendon Music and Boosey and Hawkes (ISMN M-051-21168-5).

Further reading

You can find a list of all the speech extracts in Reich's *Writings on Music: 1965–2000*.

As a whole, *Different Trains* lasts just under 27 minutes and is a type of documentary. It does not tell a story as such, but documents events through significant things that people said. Virginia and Mr David comment on the journey from Chicago to New York; the Holocaust survivors make references to events in the Holocaust. Their voices are brought together in the third movement.

Let's look at how the speech samples are used in *Different Trains*. You need to learn examples from each speaker and to think about:

➢ The pitch and range of the speech extracts

➢ The rhythms of the speech extracts

➢ How these speech extracts are used in the instrumental parts.

Virginia

Virginia has three extracts in the first movement and one in the third movement.

Her first extract is 'from Chicago to New York'. From this, we can see that her range is quite narrow, that is to say, there is not much difference between the notes. In fact, there are only two notes – F and A♭. Only two of the eight notes are A♭ and these are used to emphasise particular syllables (the middle syllable of 'Chicago' and the second syllable of 'New York').

(from   Chi - ca - go   to New Yo - rk)

Look at the rhythm of this extract. There is a slight gap between the first two words and very short rests to separate the word 'Chicago'. This shows how Reich has captured exactly the rhythm of Virginia's speech. The notes of this extract are also played (doubled) by viola 1, as Reich uses instruments of a similar pitch to the person's speech.

Mr Davis

Reich makes use of the obvious difference in pitch between the female voice of Virginia and the male voice of Mr Davis. This is Mr Davis' first speech extract in the first movement and you will see at once that it is obviously lower (bass clef rather than treble clef) and has a less regular rhythm than Virginia's extract. More importantly, the range of notes is from B to A – seven notes – and this type of speech would sound very exaggerated in real life when it was first spoken. Reich captures this exactly and it is doubled by the cello, an instrument with a similar pitch to Mr Davis' natural speaking voice.

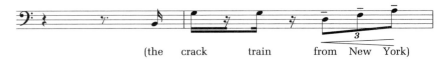

(the   crack   train   from New York)

Paul, Rachel and Rachella

Further study

The two female voices, Rachel and Rachella, are used to give a contrast in the second movement. Go through the second movement either by listening to the CD or following the score to see how Reich uses their speech extracts.

Paul's voice has a generally higher pitch than Mr Davis but is still doubled by cello. The savage nature of the invasion is captured in the way he says the word 'invaded' and this is picked up exactly in Reich's transcription.

(Ger - mans   in - va - ded   Hung - ary)

Here are three speech samples that all come in the third movement. Look at each one, play it on the keyboard and make notes about it as we have done for the examples above.

1. (Paul) 'and the war was over'

(and   the   war   was   o - ver)

2. (Mr Davis) 'from New York to Los Angeles'

(from   New   York   to   Los   An - ge - les)

3. (Rachella) 'there was one girl, who had a beautiful voice'

(there was one girl   who had a   beau-ti-ful voi-ce)

Checklist

Here is a list of some aspects of Reich's style. You need to be clear about these and apply them to the question in the examination. Don't just trot each of these out – some will be more important than others.

☑ **Autobiographical** – compares his experiences as a Jewish child travelling across America with European Jews being transported to concentration camps in the same period.

☑ **Human speech** – links back to his tape pieces in the 1960s. Uses the **speech extracts** to produce melodies.

☑ **Sampling** keyboard used (rather than tape) to record these speech extracts.

☑ Chooses extracts that are interesting and varied and which help to build up the **documentary** aspect of the piece.

☑ Use of instruments to imitate the **pitch** and **timbre** of voices.

☑ Builds up the **texture** of the piece using **counterpoint**.

☑ **Repetitive patterns** – there is no phasing, but Reich uses a number of patterns in the string parts that are not derived from the speech extracts and which simply repeat over again.

Sample examination questions

Below are three examination questions to give you an idea of the kind of question you will be asked in the exam. For the first two, we have given you some hints and tips on how to approach answering the question; for the third, we have included a full student essay, with some commentary to show you why the answer would have received an A grade.

You should try to get hold of some past papers and tackle more questions yourself, using the advice below to help you.

Web link

Past papers can be downloaded from www.ocr.org.uk.

1. **'The words of Gershwin's songs generally fit the complex rhythms of the music although sometimes the relationship seems uncomfortable'. Give examples of this from your study of Gershwin's songs and discuss the relationship between words and music in these songs.**

Understanding the question

You are being asked to cover a number of points and you need to make a plan of the structure of your answer. You will have one hour to answer the question in the examination and your answer needs to deal with these points in order:

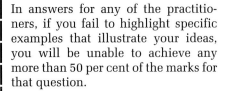

Tip

In answers for any of the practitioners, if you fail to highlight specific examples that illustrate your ideas, you will be unable to achieve any more than 50 per cent of the marks for that question.

➤ Explain that the music was written before the words.

➤ Observe that George Gershwin's melodies often have catchy rhythms that are difficult to fit words to, and that this meant there were sometimes problems in fitting lyrics to his music.

➤ From the songs you have studied, identify as many examples as you can think of where the words seem to fit the melody well – some of them are listed earlier in this chapter.

➤ Now try to think of any forced rhymes, or the subject matter changing for no reason, or cases where the song doesn't seem to be about anything – list these examples. Don't worry if you can't think of too many examples of these (although some are listed earlier) as most people agree that the Gershwins were fairly successful as a song-writing partnership.

You should conclude with a short statement confirming that this is the case.

2. **What approaches does Brecht take to structure and form in the play you have studied?**

Understanding the question

This question is fairly broad and covers a crucial aspect of the way in which Brecht designed his plays. You need plenty of examples from the play you have studied as you cover these points:

➤ Identify the overall structure of the play.

➤ Introduce the terms 'episodic' and 'epic theatre' and demonstrate how this structure works in the play.

➤ Say how far this play is episodic and the effect that Brecht creates by putting the different sections together.

➤ Think about how characters and/or plot are maintained within the overall structure.

➤ How does the timeline of the play operate?

➤ Now look at how each individual section has its own mini-structure and how Brecht works on this 'micro-level' as well as the overall plan.

➤ Think about how these sections are put together to give a moral message to the audience.

➤ Discuss any particularly comic effects produced by the structure.

➤ Consider whether Brecht gives a political message to the audience by putting the play together in this way.

3. **How does Bruce use structure and form to create dance pieces that convey poignant messages to his audience?**

Christopher Bruce uses a variety of dance forms and theatrical devices to structure his pieces. He displays a deep concern for humanity and wishes to convey this to his audience through the medium of dance. In 'Swansong' we witness the fate of a prisoner of conscience who undergoes a humiliating process of torture and interrogation at the hands of two guards.

> Addresses the question in the opening line and then goes on to indicate the essential meaning of the piece.

The piece has three sources of inspiration that lie behind the messages Bruce wishes to convey through 'Swansong': firstly the fate suffered by Chilean poet and songwriter Victor Jara, secondly the novel 'A Man' by Oriana Fallaci and thirdly Bruce's interest in Amnesty International. In order to make the audience think about his message, Bruce does not give programme notes, leaving the interpretation open. It is also possible to see 'Swansong' as representing Bruce's career and the way the piece is put together shows his own struggle between being a performer and being a director.

> Good detail concerning the stimulus for the piece, linking back to the phrase 'convey poignant messages' in the question.

The piece is divided into seven sections, which are a mixture of trios, duets and solos. Three of the sections are performed by the victim on his own. Bruce uses a variety of dance forms ranging from tap and soft-shoe to tango mixed with classical ballet movements and contemporary. This variety is typical of Bruce and his fascination for vaudeville and music hall. He uses the light-hearted approach of these art forms, but does so in a way that does not prevent the underlying message being harsh and serious. The tension builds throughout the piece and the threat of violence is always present.

> Outlines the structure of the piece and makes the crucial point about the mixture of forms in Bruce's work.

> Clearly relates form to the way in which Bruce conveys his messages.

'Swansong' is cast for three dancers and can be performed with an all male or an all female cast. Bruce specified that if the cast is mixed there must be a female and a male interrogator. He required this combination in order to keep the theme of torture and imprisonment within the realms of politics and to prevent there being a sexual dimension, so that his message is not undermined.

> Good knowledge and understanding of the casting of the piece. This is an important aspect of form.

The universal nature of the theme is important to making the audience feel that what they witness is relevant to them and therefore that Bruce's message is relevant to them. This universality is highlighted by the costume. The interrogators wear beige or light brown uniforms which indicate a military power but they display no insignia thus conveying the sense that they represent a military dictatorship anywhere in the world. The victim is dressed in a red T-shirt and jeans which could be said to represent Western culture but these clothes are available in many places across the globe, thus signifying that the prisoner could be of any nationality.

> Discussion of costume that is relevant to the message being conveyed.

The lighting in 'Swansong' is very symbolic and contributes significantly to the piece's visual structure. The audience is first faced with a bare set apart from a chair placed downstage right and about one third of the way across the stage. A light shines down on the chair from above setting the interrogation zone. A single source of light from high upstage left throws a shaft of light on a diagonal

> Discusses a key visual structural device.

Relates the staging to one of the possible messages.

towards the chair. It indicates a small window and is symbolic of escape and freedom. During his three solos, the victim works along this diagonal between the source of the shaft of light and the chair showing his desire to be free. In one sense, the chair represents Bruce's life as a performer where he feels secure and the source of light represents his new life as a choreographer. The solo sections represent his struggle to retire from performing and to continue his career in another direction, that of choreographer. The chair can be seen to be trapping him and the pain he shows in his facial expressions reflects the agonising decision he is trying to make as well as the knowledge that a dancer's life is very demanding and becomes tougher with age, particularly for one who is suffering from the long-term effects of polio.

A swansong is sung by a swan before it dies. It is also the last act of someone before they retire and both meanings are therefore

The candidate offers more than one interpretation, showing keen insight into the piece studied.

apt here. It would seem that the victim dies at the end of section seven after performing his last lyrical solo. The shaft of light is lowered so that the victim's shadow lengthens across the stage. The light fades and the overhead light shows the interrogators staring at the empty chair. There is a poignant message as the light can represent a new life for the victim. If he is dead, then his spirit is free and the torture must cease.

Relates the composition of the music to the structure of the piece and its poignancy.

The music is significant in the structuring of the piece as well as in the setting of the atmosphere and the changes in mood. Chambon used a variety of sounds to create an atmospheric score for the piece. The atmosphere and mood are crucial to making the audience feel that the messages are poignant and being truly affected by them. The music is electro-acoustic and comprises original, sampled and digitally reproduced sounds. These include the grating metal of kitchen pans as well as soft vocalising and the rhythms of popular dance forms. To add contrast and to increase tension some of the dance is performed in silence. The structure of the score helps to outline the structure of the piece. The piece

Contrast and tension are key elements of structure. Good detail here concerning the musical composition method.

begins with the victim sitting on a chair stage right and then the interrogators enter. They always enter from stage right, which indicates that this is the position of the door of the cell. Before the music begins they perform a short tap sequence which bonds them together and shows that they will work as a team. The piece starts off in a light-hearted manner but then an electronic crash signals a change of mood and the atmosphere becomes heavy with anticipation of the torture to come.

Unison work is used by the interrogators to show that they are a strong unit. The victim has to imitate their moves or tap out answers to their questions. The interrogators play a game of cat-and-mouse with the victim and humiliate him as trios, duets and solos are used and the victim struggles to keep up with the pace. The victim's movement vocabulary includes phrases with

The candidate mentions some of the movement vocabulary used by Bruce, and explains how the dance forms in the piece are used to create the humiliation and struggles of the victim, which is one of the aspects Bruce wants to get across to his audience.

arabesques, leaps and open-arm gestures indicating a desire to fly away. The section ends as it begins with the victim sitting on the chair thus showing the circularity of the game and the monotony and predictability of the victim's predicament.

Fallaci describes the process of torture and interrogation as being like a 'theatrical production' where people enter and exit according to instructions. The interrogators are like characters, each of whom has a different role but a single purpose: to make the victim talk. Bruce's use of the various dance forms emphasises this.

In 'Swansong', Bruce shows the interrogators trying to make the victim talk by using a variety of methods, represented by different dance and drama forms. For example, they use commedia dell' arte where improvisation and comedy give a light-hearted feel to the piece while a serious message is being delivered. In Section Two, 'Tea for Two', a red nose is placed on the victim and the interrogators perform an amusing soft-shoe tango-style duet. The victim has to join in and the dance becomes increasingly more aggressive. Violence is indicated as kicks and hitting are used. No bodily harm is done to the victim on stage but the power of suggestion through the strong dynamic of the movement is extremely effective. As the tension increases throughout the piece, we see the victim becoming more nervous. He visibly flinches at the beginning of Section Four as the first interrogator reaches him.

> Relates back to the question.

The audience is lulled into a false sense of security as an adagio section begins and the victim is supported in a trio of low motion lifts and holds. This seeming kindness on the part of the interrogators does not last and soon they are throwing and pushing him about the stage, using the chair as a weapon against him and at one time holding him upside-down above it as if his head is being held under water. The forms used by the dancers reflect their characters and attitudes in a powerful way.

> This paragraph demonstrates excellent knowledge and understanding of the content of the piece and how this relates to the overall themes and messages of 'Swansong'.

In Section Six, music hall and vaudeville styles are used as the interrogators perform a soft-shoe dance with their canes. The

tempo picks up as the canes become weapons and are then discarded. A group dance takes place which uses movement material from other sections of the piece. The victim becomes exhausted and collapses. His tired body is placed on the chair and the interrogators look annoyed as they can no longer play with him. This clearly conveys the cruelty of the interrogators and their lack of regard for the victim.

Juxtaposed with the group sections are the victim's three solos with their contrasting lyrical feel. The first solo starts with what sounds like a scream and the victim stretches his arms out, unclenching his fists. He crouches and turns to the side with his back and arms curved in a bird-like position, making him look like a defenceless animal. The dancer's centre of gravity is low and his pliés are deep. He uses off-centre balances, flexed feet and contractions with slow movement in the style of Graham to express his inner pain. Contrasted with this heavy movement are arabesques, attitudes and outstretched arms which are used like wings. This lighter movement conveys the victim's desire to be free

> Good discussion of movement content and different dance forms. It also goes on to explain what these convey to the audience.

like a bird and is used in the other two solos. Quicker and small intricate steps performed in a cramped circular floor pattern are used to show how small the cell is and how the victim feels trapped.

In Section Five, the chair is used to show how trapped the victim feels as he holds it in front of him like bars, then stands on it and becomes shackled by it as his feet are trapped in it. The autobiographical nature of the piece is perhaps clearest in this section.

The last solo in Section Seven is more poignant as the interrogators are on stage and looking at the chair as if the victim's corpse lies there. The victim dances along the diagonal shaft of light and eventually leaves in the direction of the source of the light,

Here the candidate directly addresses the question again.

which indicates that the struggle is over. He smiles as he looks back on his prison indicating that the struggle is over and giving a sense of hope to the piece.

Using an almost bare set, simple lighting, atmospheric music together with a small cast performing a mixture of dance styles enhanced with dramatic delivery Bruce gives his audience much food for thought. He raises their awareness of the injustice of the treatment of prisoners of conscience wherever they may be. He does not tell the audience what crime the victim is accused of, nor which regime is holding him prisoner. We do not know whether he is innocent or guilty but we have witnessed the brutal treatment he suffers at the hands of his guards and we have been made to think and perhaps act. Bruce has achieved the delivery of a poignant message to his audience through using a variety of forms and styles and a clear episodic structure to his piece.

In the concluding paragraph, the candidate gives an effective summary of the points made in the essay about the structure and form of the piece and the possible messages conveyed.

The essay is clearly structured and covers the key aspects of the question. There is good depth of analysis, and impressive knowledge and understanding of the piece studied. It is well written, with no spelling or grammar mistakes.

Tip

Don't feel daunted by the length of this essay – it is meant as a useful guide, rather than as a strict template. The examiners are well aware of the time constraints you are under in the exam, and it is certainly possible to achieve an A grade in a more concise essay than this, as long as relevant points are made and supported by appropriate references to the piece. It is the quality of what you write that is more important than the quantity, and it is vital that you spend time at the beginning of the exam planning your answer, rather than diving straight in and writing page after page of unstructured waffle.

Performance Realisation

In the first unit, Language of Performing Arts, you devised and performed four original pieces – but whereas there you were assessed on your written commentary, in this unit you will be assessed on your abilities as a performer. This is your opportunity to show off the performance skills you have learned during the AS course – it may well be the moment you've been waiting for!

You will take part in two performances either on your own or in a group of no more than seven people. You do not need to be in the same groups for both pieces, so you could do a solo piece for one performance and a group piece for the second. On the other hand, if you work well with a group for one piece, you may wish to work with the same group for the second piece, as you'll be able to support each other in both pieces.

The length of each piece is related to how many people are taking part: about three minutes for every person in the group. If it is a solo, your performance must be about three minutes long. If seven people are performing, the total length of the performance may be as long as 21 minutes. However, even if there are seven people in your group, you are unlikely to need the full 21 minutes, as your performances will overlap. Each person must have three minutes' exposure so that the examiner has time to assess each of you properly, but if you are all on stage at once, then the total playing time of the piece can be cut down. Think carefully about the length of your piece, since it can be very difficult to sustain the energy and interest if it goes on too long and it may be better to keep it concise.

The performances that you create will be related to the works you studied for the Contextual Studies unit. This is an important aspect, as examiners will expect your performances to show that you have a good understanding of the style of the practitioners you've learnt about.

One of your performances will be a piece of repertoire; the other an original devised piece. The important thing to remember at this stage is that in both you will be assessed on your performance skills. You need to make sure that each piece is as good as the other, since otherwise your result for the unit will not reflect your true potential. Make sure that you rehearse both pieces thoroughly using the techniques you learnt when studying for the Language of Performing Arts unit.

How to approach the performances

When preparing your performance pieces, there are three important questions that you need to ask:

➤ What performance skills do I need in both pieces?

➤ What is the best way to approach repertoire?

➤ How should I go about devising an original piece?

Tip

You need to think carefully about whether to work in the same group for both pieces, in different groups, or do either or both of them as a solo. Discuss this with your tutor and see which would work best for you.

Timings

It is best if you are able to read through this section before you start your practical work but even if you have already begun, you can still benefit by checking that you have not missed anything important.

Performance space

Performance skills for both pieces

Whether you are performing a piece of repertoire or your own devised piece, there are a number of generic (general) performance skills that you should demonstrate and aspects to consider. That is to say, there are some elements that you would expect to find in any successful piece of performance work and in many ways these are more important than the specifics of the piece. For example, while you may have devised a piece that is an excellent example of your chosen practitioner's style, if you cannot perform it without breaking down, you will not achieve very much credit, because the good will be overshadowed by the bad.

This is a vital aspect to get right to ensure that you can demonstrate your performance skills to your best ability. It really does matter where you choose to perform! A classroom with the desks pushed aside for you to sing a song will look cluttered and give the impression that you cannot be bothered to make the performance space look professional. It sounds obvious, but you need to choose a performance space that is big enough for the performance. Similarly, think about where you want the audience to sit or stand in your performance space.

In reality, you may not have very much choice over the space in which you perform. It will probably take place in your dance, drama or music studio, the main assembly hall or your school or college theatre if you have one. You should have some choice over how you position the audience for the performance and you should think carefully about how much space you need to perform before deciding where the audience will sit.

Consider the following issues when deciding on the layout of the performance space:

➢ How close to the audience do you want to be?

If you are too close, it could be intimidating for both you and the audience. If you are performing in a large group, it may be difficult for audience members sitting close to you to get a feel for what everyone in the piece is doing. If the audience is too far away, they will probably feel alienated from the piece and may not be able to hear or see clearly what is going on.

➢ How do you want the seats for the audience to be arranged?

You may simply want the audience to sit in rows facing the front – effectively a traditional proscenium arch style. If you are performing in a space that has fixed seating, you may have little choice but to go for this approach. However, in a studio space, or even in a larger hall, you have the option of performing in the round or in any other arrangement appropriate to the style of the performance. Consider the advantages and disadvantages of the following types of performance space: theatre **in the round**, **thrust stage**, **end-on stage** and **traverse stage**.

Remember that the examiner has to have a good view of the piece and should be slightly away from the audience. This may influence your decision about how to position the audience.

➢ How do you want the piece to be lit?

It is normally more effective if the performance uses stage lighting. If you do not have any stage lighting available, you may perform in daylight or using the normal light available in the room.

If you decide to light your piece, you must do it effectively. Do not make the whole piece too dark (the rules about contrast apply). Make sure that you rehearse in the light that you have chosen for the performance. Imagine the frustration that the audience will experience if the piece appears gloomy and slow all the way through.

What generic performance skills do you need to demonstrate? The following list is not exhaustive but you can use it as a check list for your performance.

The most important thing about your performance is that it is fluent: it needs to keep going. One of the most distracting things for an audience is a performance breaking down, and this is the aspect most likely to stick in their minds once the piece has ended. If your piece has any slips at all in it, this means that your performance memory is not sufficiently developed. You must learn your part off by heart so that there is absolutely no hint of hesitation or stumbling. We all know that rehearsing a piece can be tedious if you go over the same thing time and time again. But it is the only way to make sure that everyone is completely certain of what they have to do in the piece.

Fluency

Tip

If you're having difficulty remembering part of a devised piece, don't keep changing it each time you rehearse it. Agree on what it should be and stick to that.

Tempo is the next most important element, since a performance that is fluent but has no contrast or pacing is not going to impress an audience. Ask yourself how much contrast each of your pieces has. Does the whole piece move at the same tempo? Is it too fast (too many things happening at too quick a pace) or too slow (everything is spelled out in huge detail so the piece never gets any energy)? A successful piece will contain some sections that are more intense than others and you will be able to balance the energy levels between difference sections.

Tempo and contrast

Tip

Use a metronome to check the pace of your piece and see what contrasts of tempo it has. If you find that in your piece, the metronome beat is the same all the way through, you need to work on varying the sections.

Anyone who watches or listens to a performance wants to feel engaged with what is going on. There are some straightforward ways of making sure that your audience feels this and enjoys what you are presenting.

Commitment

Think of your performance as a conversation between two friends. If one person talks very quickly and loudly, hardly pausing for breath, then the second person will start to lose interest. The same is likely to happen if one person speaks very slowly, always at the same pitch and tone.

You need to be careful that your role in the performance does not create either of these effects. The most important thing is that you allow your performance to breathe – there need to be some points when things move along rapidly, balanced by other points when the action pauses or there is time for reflection.

Further study

Watch a video of your performance and make a map of where the high points and low points come. This will also be useful when you think about the structure – does the overall shape of the piece work, or are some sections too long or too short?

Be aware of your eyes, voice, demeanour, posture and movement. There are some essential things to remember here. The most

Using the body

obvious is that you are going to perform live so you will almost certainly have to communicate through your body. Some students get very nervous about this and as a result do not give their best performance on the day of the exam. Here are some dos and don'ts about how to use your body:

☑ **Warm up your body thoroughly before you start any practical work.**

This is as important if you are playing the flute as if you are taking part in a piece of physical theatre. If you try to jump into performance work when you are not prepared for it, your body may well not work as you would like it to. Have a look at the section on pages 29–30 about exploring physicality – you must feel comfortable in your body if you are going to give your best performance.

☑ **Occupy your space with confidence.**

Stand properly and don't slouch! It is surprising how difficult many people find it to stand in a natural, relaxed manner. This follows on from the previous point – you need to be comfortable in your body before you can hope to stand well or occupy your space effectively. Watch out for two errors in particular: one is standing rigid in the same spot as if you have been turned into stone (singers beware!); the second is wandering aimlessly around the performance space with no real focus or intention. Both of these will probably irritate the audience and make the examiner wonder about what you intended to communicate through your performance.

☑ **Prepare your face.**

Your facial expressions during the performance will communicate a lot to your audience. Think about some of the tell-tale signs of nervousness – swallowing hard, frowning, squinting, eyes flitting around and so on. Even if your performance is fluent and your technique is secure, you may lose several marks if your face tells the audience that you are not enjoying the performance. Practise with a mirror. If you have a dance background, you will be quite used to this. If you have a drama or music background then using a mirror may seem strange at first but you will quickly get used to it. By practising with a mirror you will see the same expressions your audience will see. Do you like the effect? If not, practise until you do!

☑ **Prepare your voice.**

If you are taking part in a dance piece, there may not be any dialogue. In drama or music performances, you will generally need to use your voice. In drama, you need to be able to control your **diction** and shape your lines. In music, you need to prepare your voice to make sure it has good resonance – even if you decide to use a microphone for the performance. Whatever art form you are working in, don't forget to breathe! If you cannot control your breathing, your voice will not do what you want it to and you will either sound breathless or sluggish.

⌧ **Fiddling during the performance.**

Everyone has some irritating habits that may surface when performing. For example, you may bite your nails, blink frequently, fiddle with your hair or play with your costume. Any of these can be intensely distracting for an audience. The audience wants to focus on the performance image you are trying to create and do not want to be put off by irritating gestures or mannerisms.

Have an honesty session with your fellow students. Use it as a game and try to find one thing about each person that you think they are not aware of. You all need to agree to trust one another in this session and not to be negative just for the sake of it. Remember that the idea of the exercise is to help one another become more self-aware and therefore more able to create a role external to your own personality.

There are no specific marks for the way you look in your performance but it goes without saying that you want to look the part and create the right impression.

Performance studies is all about being able to assume a particular role in performance and this role might be quite different from your natural instincts and persona. For example, if you are performing a set of songs by George Gershwin, then wearing ripped jeans, trainers and a tatty T-shirt is unlikely to enhance the performance! If you want the look of the performance to reinforce what you are doing, you need to think about what would be the best thing to wear.

You need to consider the dynamic of your group. If both of your pieces are individual, this issue is obviously of less relevance, but if you're performing in a group, you will need to support the other members of the group – whether there are only two or as many as seven of you. One of the greatest temptations is to concentrate only on getting a good mark for yourself at the expense of considering the others. If you take this approach you will almost certainly ruin it for everyone, as you will make the piece unbalanced. You need to start by being determined that everyone in the group must do the very best they can.

In performing, you need to be generous. That means you need to be aware of the status of each person in the performance and what they are doing at any particular point. If you are to be generous in your approach, you will take a lead when it is appropriate and you will support at other times. That way, you will make a full contribution to the ensemble and demonstrate that you fully understand the changing dynamics of the performance.

How to approach repertoire

This unit requires you to perform work by established practitioners as well as work that you have devised yourself. This is demanding and will require a good level of performance skills. We are going to focus first of all on how to approach performing a piece of repertoire and then discuss how you should go about devising your own material.

What to wear

Also think about any body piercings you have, as these might detract from the performance and, in the case of physical theatre, could pose a health and safety issue. As noted in the Introduction, tongue piercings can affect voice production and therefore clarity and diction. Facial piercings will affect communication with the audience and make your character less believable – in all three art forms.

Group interaction and dynamics

Tip

Look out for 'passengers' – those not very committed to the performance process, not reliable at turning up and unlikely to contribute very much when they are there – and prima donnas – those who want to hog the limelight and dominate the whole piece, convinced that their performance skills are better than everyone else's. If you are concerned about your group's dynamics, seek advice from your tutor, who may act as mediator in an open group session. This will allow you to share your concerns without personalising them and help the group move forward in a more positive way to a more successful end result.

Whether your piece of repertoire is taken from dance, drama or music, there are a number of things you need to do to ensure that your performance is successful. Here are 12 key points to help you get the best mark you can.

1.   Choose an extract of repertoire that is appropriate for the group's interests, skills and abilities.

Your repertoire piece for this unit will be the work – or an extract from it – that you studied in depth for one of the practitioners in the Contextual Studies unit. In a long work, it can be difficult to know exactly which extract to perform so it's best to make sure you've read through, listened to or watched the whole piece, so that you gain some insight in to what it might look or sound like before you make any decisions.

You need to be realistic about your individual abilities and what you believe you can achieve as a group. While there is no point in choosing an extract that is considerably beyond your ability or that of most of the group, you need to make sure that the extract or piece is challenging enough for you to be able to show the skills you have, otherwise, it is likely to get stale very quickly.

2.   Agree as a group what role each person should take.

While it's natural to want the main role in a piece, it's actually more important that you take a role that best demonstrates your abilities. It doesn't matter if you are not central to the whole piece as long as you have enough to do and as long as what you do allows you to show your abilities during the piece. The most important thing is to make sure you have the right amount of exposure to make your contribution count.

3.   Agree how long the extract should be – make cuts sensitively so that the piece does not lose its impact.

Your piece needs to allow each person to have three minutes' exposure, up to the maximum length of 21 minutes for a group of seven candidates. Discuss what length would enable every member of the group to have the appropriate amount of exposure, while still keeping the performance focused.

Be careful and sensitive when making cuts and choosing an extract, so that you still manage to convey the impact of the piece.

4.   Look at the list of fingerprints for each practitioner: these are the specific aspects that must be obvious to your audience.

You might think that this is important only if you are devising your own piece, but it's important here too. You need to be completely aware of the practitioner's style as you perform. If you're not, your performance may not look or sound like the real thing, even if it is technically correct.

5.   Decide on the method of working most appropriate to your chosen art form.

Although it is in the nature of performance studies to investigate links between the art forms, it is important to recognise that there are also differences and that these are often quite significant.

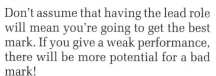

Tip

If there are several groups in your class, why not arrange for each group to perform a different extract so that the examiner will see a performance of most – or all – of the piece? On the day of the performance, make sure that the groups perform in the right order so that the piece follows through!

Tip

Don't assume that having the lead role will mean you're going to get the best mark. If you give a weak performance, there will be more potential for a bad mark!

Tip

Look back over your notes on your chosen practitioners for the Contextual Studies unit. Remind yourself of the style of the piece you are performing and memorise all the stylistic fingerprints of the practitioner.

Dance is usually recorded on video and, in some cases, in notation as well. There are two systems of dance notation – Laban and Benesh – and the two are quite different. In addition, a considerable number of dancers do not regularly use either of these systems. Where performances of existing works take place, they are either taught to the dancers or recreated from videos of existing performances. If you are involved in recreating a piece of dance repertoire, a combination of these is likely to be the case for you: you should have access to a video of the piece and your tutor will also direct you in class.

Drama performances are occasionally recorded, but the most common method is to buy a printed copy of the play. The role of the actors and the director is therefore to translate from page to stage. If you are involved in recreating a piece of existing drama repertoire, you will have to make the text work in performance and you will have to adopt a **directorial concept** of what you intend to achieve in your performance of this extract. Since plays tend to be longer than either dance or music pieces, you will need to think carefully about how to select an appropriate extract.

Music performances are sometimes based on printed music notation, and are sometimes **cover versions** of songs by established artists. If a number of recorded performances are available, you will be able to compare these with the written notation to get a feel for different ways of interpreting the piece. If you are involved in performing a piece of music repertoire, try to get hold of a CD recording and the music notation.

Web link

For a simple introduction to Labanotation, try www.dancenotation.org/lnbasics/frame0.html, and for more details on Benesh notation, visit www.benesh.org.

6. **Map the structure of the piece and, if it is an extract, make sure you know what happens before and after.**

You need to have a full understanding of the piece you're performing. In the Contextual Studies unit, we suggested you make a diagram of the structure of the piece to help you prepare for the written examination, and it will prove useful here too. So if you haven't already done so, make a chart of how the piece is put together and make sure you understand where the climax points are. This way you'll be able to make some contrasts with the more relaxed parts of the piece.

See page 52.

7. **Run through the whole piece or extract as soon as possible so that you have a feel for how it works.**

You need to do a run-through as soon as you are able. You can work on individual sections to improve them, but you need to be able to see the extent of the task before you so that you know where the work is going to need to be done.

Tip

When you first run through your piece, time it. Aim to time it once a week. Every week, it should take a little less time as you improve your skills.

8. **Everyone in the piece should be allowed to act as director for a session.**

It's easy to criticise but it's hard to do so effectively. There is no place for negative or personal criticism during your rehearsals, but there are some very critical questions that you need to ask. Why not allow everyone a chance to act as director for one session? This means that one person watches the latest video recording of your piece in rehearsal and then directs the next session. Remember, though, that this is not media studies: don't be influenced by the

Tip

Make a video at the end of each week so that you can see whether the performance is getting better. If it isn't, ask yourselves honestly why it isn't and what you can do to remedy this.

video alone. Ask other people to watch the piece and say what they think.

Here are some helpful questions to ask:

☑ Is the piece the right length? Does every member of the group have the right amount of exposure?

☑ Is the piece interesting to watch?

☑ Are there effective contrasts in the performance or is it all on the same level?

☑ Is the balance of the sound right?

☑ If you are using lighting, how effective is it?

☑ If there are transitions in the piece, are they effective?

☑ How much does it look or sound like the original?

☒ Are some roles under-exposed (we don't see enough of them) or over-exposed (they dominate the piece)?

9. Rehearse – rehearse – rehearse.

You may find it tiresome having to go through the same piece time and time again, but your piece will only be the best it can be if you rehearse rigorously and often. You need to know exactly what happens in the piece so that you can perform it without having to think about it. In other words, you need to develop your performance memory. One of the worst things that can happen in a performance is for the piece to break down – this is very unsettling for both performer and audience.

10. Make sure you have a dress rehearsal.

It is essential to have a dress rehearsal in which you run through the piece exactly as you intend it to be on the day of the examination. During this rehearsal you need to have the same performance discipline as you will in the real performance. In other words, you need to warm up, compose yourselves and focus – and ignore anything that does not go exactly as you wanted.

11. Write programme notes.

Don't forget to write programme notes for your audience and your examiner. These should be attractively presented (not handwritten) and give the impression that you are about to give a professional and well-rehearsed performance. The examiner **must** receive this information two weeks prior to the exam.

12. On the day of performance.

On the day of the performance there will be a couple of things that you will not have done before. Firstly, there will be a short interview with the examiner, which, in the case of a repertoire performance, is unlikely to last long. The questions will cover the role you have taken, the nature of the piece, the aspects of the practitioner's style that you hope to bring out and any other relevant features of the piece. The discussion is not assessed, so relax and be confident.

Secondly, you will have to say your name and candidate number on video before you perform. Some candidates get embarrassed about this and may laugh or look ill at ease. This can be disastrous, as it breaks your performance preparation and you may lose

See pages 9 and 111 on what to wear.

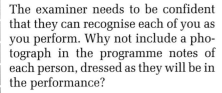

Tip

The examiner needs to be confident that they can recognise each of you as you perform. Why not include a photograph in the programme notes of each person, dressed as they will be in the performance?

concentration. Practise saying your name and candidate number confidently, with a smile and with no sense of self-consciousness.

So, breathe, relax and perform. By now you should know the piece inside out – be confident!

How to approach devising

There are two essential aspects to what the examiner will be looking for in your performance of the devised piece, and these will determine what mark you get for your work. The aspects can be summarised in two questions:

➢ Does this piece look or sound like the work of the practitioner the candidate has studied?

➢ How good is the candidate's level of performance skills?

In some ways, the second part is harder than the first. A lot of what we have said about preparing to perform a piece of repertoire is also true of performing your own piece. You need the same high level of performance skills and the same disciplined, methodical approach to preparing and rehearsing the piece. The new feature is that you have to put together your own material and this can be a real challenge.

So what should you do in devising your piece to make the most of your abilities and get the best mark? The following points build on what we said earlier about performance realisation.

It may sound obvious, but if you are going to succeed in producing a piece in the style of the practitioner you've studied, you need to have a very good idea of what that style is. Have a look at the list of main points about each practitioner on pages 64, 70, 78, 85, 95 and 101. If you don't understand what these are, it is absolutely vital that you do not yet start devising your own piece.

If you're performing in a group, then the same goes for every member – you all need to have a shared understanding of the style you are trying to create before you start.

One of the most common mistakes is to focus on the 'story' of the piece rather than the style – the Holocaust or separation of parents for Reich's *Different Trains*, war for Brecht's *Mother Courage*, South America for Bruce's *Ghost Dances* and so on. Avoid these temptations! The practitioners are important in the world of performing arts because of their style rather as social historians.

Once you have done this, you can think of an appropriate theme for the piece, but remember that some pieces are not really about anything. If you've studied Reich's *Piano Phase*, for example, you'll recall that the technique of the piece is the only thing that really matters and there is no story as such. You don't *have* to have a story – in some cases you could simply have a structure that explores aspects of technique. In most cases, however, the story will be necessary to keep the interest of your audience. Choose carefully though, and try to avoid going for obvious or tired themes.

The same rules apply as for the repertoire performance: your piece needs to allow each candidate to have three minutes' exposure. As

Tip

First impressions count. If you stumble over saying your name and candidate number, you may give the examiner the advance impression that your performance is going to be embarrassed and awkward.

Tip

It's a good idea to work on your repertoire piece first. You'll be assessed on your level of performance skills in both pieces so why not start work on performing an extract of someone else's work before you have to start devising yourself?

Knowing the style

Tip

If you misunderstand the style of your practitioner, you will not do well in the examination even if your performance is of a high standard.

Tip

If you're working in a group, spend time when you first get together discussing the fingerprints of the practitioner you are studying. Try out some practical exercises to explore how you could demonstrate this style.

Length and structure

before, you do not have to perform for the maximum length of time and you will almost certainly find that your marks are better if you keep the piece well focused.

When working on the repertoire piece, you made a map of the piece's structure in order to understand how it fitted together. Here you must do the opposite – draw a structure that you think will work and that you can work around. Look back at the section on form and structure in the Language of Performing Arts chapter. Using one of these as the basis of your devised piece would give you a ready-made structure to work from. Of course, if the piece that you have studied has a particular structure, you could simply use that as the basis of your piece. If you are devising a song in the style of Gershwin, you could take a chord progression and the tempo of a song as your basis, and compose a new set of words and a new melody. This would ensure that some elements were identical but not the most obvious ones.

See page 15.

Improvise–Rehearse–Perform

Also crucial to the Language of Performing Arts unit was the structured process of improvising–rehearsing–performing. You need to follow the same process again now. Once you have agreed on a structure, developed your ideas and have the piece assembled, you need to rehearse, and keep on rehearsing until everyone knows their role in the piece off by heart without any hesitation. You will find that performance memory is as important in devised work as in performing repertoire.

Look back at what we said about rehearsal on pages 15–16 to see how important it is.

You need to produce professional-looking, helpful programme notes that help the examiner and your audience understand what you are trying to do in the piece. These should be sent by your teacher with your candidate photos to the examiner two weeks before the exam.

On the day, your discussion with the examiner will take longer for the devised piece, as they'll need to know exactly what you've done before they watch the performance. Remember the two main points about the assessment: do you understand the practitioner's style and can you perform to a good standard?

Tip

Remember to invite an audience. Examiners like to be part of an audience when they watch the performance. Watching alone can be a very lonely experience, especially if you want the audience to respond. However, don't try to involve the examiner in the performance – they're not allowed to speak or take part.

Dance

There are a number of general performance skills that you need in order to perform dance repertoire from either Bruce or Newson, as well as considerations about what will be suitable for you.

Do you have the necessary skills?

It may sound obvious, but if you choose to perform a solo then you must make sure it is one that you are capable of performing. Remember that the dancers at the Rambert Dance Company train every day and dance many hours each day. Consequently they have very strong muscles and excellent flexibility so that they can perform the demanding and challenging arabesques, balances and turns from a piece such as *Swansong*. Equally, one of the traits of Newson's work is the demanding physicality and the risk-taking that the members of DV8 undertake. Talk to your teacher before making any decisions and make sure that you will be physically capable of performing the extract that you have chosen by the time the examination comes round.

What do you want to communicate to the audience when you perform this piece? How do you want to make them feel? Watch the extract that you have chosen to perform several times on video in order to get the feel of it. Write down in bullet-point form how it makes you feel as an audience member and, if performing in a group, discuss with other members what each of you wrote. Go back to these notes once you've learnt the piece and ask another member of your class or a friend or family member to watch you perform. Ask them how they feel after watching it and note down their comments. Have you communicated effectively with your audience?

The set should be kept simple and only essential props should be used. Discuss the lighting with your teacher or technician well in advance of the exam so that you can rehearse with it as a familiar part of your performance. The technician will also need time to experiment and set this up for you.

You can wear jazz shoes or be barefoot. If you have long hair, make sure that it is tied back. Never fiddle with your costume, hair or props on stage as it will detract from your performance and irritate the examiner.

Make sure that you have your own copy of the music and that the technician or teacher has a copy. Listen to the music on a daily basis so that you know it off by heart. Rehearse with the sound technician so that they know when to start the music and when to fade it out if this is necessary.

The volume at which the music is played is also very important, as you do not want to let the music dominate the dance. Run a sound check before the performances begin so that the music is at the correct level. Do not have the music too loud for the audience nor too soft for the performers. Run the sound check with the performers on stage and a teacher or another performer in the auditorium to check sound levels at various positions in the space. Remember to check sound for the video recording as well.

Map out the movements on the floor of your performance space and make sure that it is safe for you to perform them on the floor, which should be sprung. Watch the video to make sure that you are performing on the right lines and in the right areas of the stage. Use the nine areas of the stage diagram featured in the introduction to this guide and plot the pathways on to the grid.

You must work with a pulse or counts when you rehearse. When you perform the piece for your examination, you may feel nervous and consequently rush the piece. If you have rehearsed regularly using counts in your head and listening to the soundtrack, then you should be able to perform the piece in time with the music. Look carefully at the pace of the piece and how it changes. Use a metronome when counting the beats for each movement.

Having said your name to camera, take a deep breath, relax and start to focus on the performance. You should have warmed up

Communication

Setting the stage

Think about...
If your school/college cannot provide the lighting effects you need, how might you get round the problem using natural light?

Climaxes, pathways and pace

See page 11.

Beginning and ending

beforehand and now be prepared to perform. If you have had technical and dress rehearsals, you should be feeling confident. Take up your starting position on stage and remain still. The lights should be brought down and then up as a signal for you to start. The music should start and you begin.

If there is a problem with your costume, hair or a prop during the performance, just carry on as if nothing has happened. You will be credited for not being distracted by the problem. If there is a technical problem beyond your control, you may be allowed to perform the piece again. The rule is that whatever goes wrong, carry on until the end, or until the examiner asks you to stop.

The end of a performance can be an uncomfortable moment for the audience and the examiner if the performer does not give a signal to show that the piece has finished. In the case of the victim's solo in Bruce's *Swansong*, the dancer might walk off, following the shaft of light from upstage left. The lights should then go down and the audience will start to clap. The dancer does not need to come back to take a bow but can do if this has been rehearsed with the technician. The dancer walks to the front of the stage and looks up, arms by their sides, and bows with head bent down, and then straightens to a normal standing position while looking out to the audience. The dancer then walks or runs (not too fast!) off stage left or right depending on the type of facility you have.

Choosing your repertoire

Group or solo?

One of the most fundamental decisions you will have to make when choosing what to perform is whether you wish to perform with others in a group or perform a solo.

If you are performing a solo, it should be about three minutes in duration – you may find that you have to cut it slightly if you choose one that is longer. Look for a convenient place in the piece that seems appropriate and make sure that it will still make sense to an audience. Remember to cut the music as well, or be aware of where to fade it out at the end. If you are working in a group, the length of the piece will depend on how many people are in the group and to what extent you are all on stage at the same time. Again, choose an extract that works well in isolation with suitable beginning and end points.

Performing repertoire by Bruce

If you want to perform from a Bruce piece as a group, you will probably choose one or two sections to ensure that everyone has equal exposure. Time the sections of *Ghost Dances* and look for appropriate sections for the number of dancers in your group. In *Swansong*, you have the option of duets and a trio, but, again, you must time the sections. The timings of the music tracks are given on the CD and would prove useful when choosing sections to perform.

Working on a solo

Let's say that you've decided on a solo from Bruce's *Swansong*. Here are some guidelines that will help you to produce a polished performance.

Setting your stage. In order to perform the solo properly, you will need a chair placed in the correct position on the stage and a shaft of light representing the window or freedom coming from high upstage left. Depending on which solo you choose, the light source may be moved down to elongate your shadow.

Using a pulse. Since you're performing on your own, the onus is entirely on you to keep in time. You can use climaxes in the music or sound effects to see where certain movements appear in the piece. Use a pulse to count as you perform each movement so that you are in time with the music and do not race ahead, finishing the solo a long time before the music finishes. The danger is that you will rush or change the pace each time you perform the piece. Look, for instance, at the beginning when the victim has just left the chair and is crouching down with his arms held bent and behind him looking like a bird. This is a very slow movement. Count how many beats, with or without the use of a metronome.

The imaginary line between the chair and the shaft of light. *Swansong* demands a lot of precision and careful placement. Having mapped out the pathways, it should be easier to see the line from the chair to the direction of the shaft of light. You could rehearse with a chalk line on the floor and work along it. When you perform the piece without the chalk line, the audience should be able to perceive the line as you perform the movements along it and in the two directions – towards the chair or towards the light. You need to be clear in your head what the chair and the light symbolise at this moment in the piece. You should be yearning for the light, forever stretching towards it trying to find freedom, but finding that the chair is holding you back. Rehearse the balletic movements along the line and work on strengthening the balances. The arabesque, for example, needs to be held and almost suspended. You need to create a contrast between the held positions and falling into the next movement.

What to wear. Clothing is quite simple for the victim – a red T-shirt and a pair of stretch jeans. The material for the jeans must be able to stretch in order for you to be able to use your full flexibility.

Devising in the style of Bruce

For devising in the style of Bruce, consider the following elements of his work and how you can incorporate some of his fingerprints into your own piece.

You may wish to tackle a specific issue in your devised dance piece. In creating his works, Bruce is inspired by causes that are, for example, political or environmental. He looks at humanity and how people are oppressed by those in power, and tries to make his pieces have universal appeal.

What do you consider to be of significance in the world today? What do you feel passionate about? Read through the newspapers and watch TV news and documentaries to find something happening in the world that makes you angry. You need to find an issue that you feel is being ignored and that you feel you could make an audience aware of using the medium of dance. Bruce's

Subject matter

Remember the warning on page 115 not to take the story as your influence. It is acceptable to take the fact that Bruce was inspired by causes he felt strongly about as inspiration, just not a cause or event that he has already employed. So you can use dance to express your ideas on something that you're passionate about, but you should not devise a piece about South America simply because that was Bruce's starting point for *Swansong* and *Ghost Dances*.

pieces often have an international dimension, so think broadly before decided on a starting point. Some ideas might be:

➤ Child labour

➤ Domestic violence

➤ Asylum seekers.

Styles

You may find that your choice of subject matter has some obvious impact on the styles you choose to incorporate into your piece. You can use folk dance but create your own steps as Bruce did for *Ghost Dances* if this is relevant to your piece.

What's crucial in adhering to Bruce's techniques is to use a variety of styles, in particular a fusion of classical and contemporary. Which other dance styles might you use? You need to decide why you have chosen the styles and what you are trying to communicate through them. Consider ballroom dances or other social dances you might use. Use some unison work. Look again in the piece you have studied to see how Bruce used this compositional device.

Think about how Bruce uses humour to deliver a serious message to the audience. How might you incorporate elements of commedia dell'arte, music hall, vaudeville or clowning into your piece? What might you use them to achieve?

Movement

Think about Bruce's use of intricate footwork, circles and chain patterns as well as step sequences that move in a sideways direction. How could you incorporate a flexible torso and spiralling movements? Since Bruce is known for inventing new steps, you could even try inventing some of your own.

Create gestures that are appropriate for your theme. Remember the bird-like motifs in *Swansong* representing the swan both in flight and crouching on the ground, and the animalistic movement of the ghost dancers.

Watch the Bruce piece that you have studied one more time. Consider how he uses pathways on the stage as well as exits and entrances. Look carefully at how he uses levels and how he groups dancers in a variety of ways. Where are they placed on stage and how do they relate to other sets of characters? What do they do when they are not the main focus of attention in the piece?

Structure

Bruce's pieces are often episodic in structure, broken down into sections, each of which tells a certain story or provides a flashback giving insight into a character's life or relationship with another character. The sections build to a climax and are juxtaposed with each other in order to create statements relating to the theme of the piece or the serious underlying issue. The ending is often left open to interpretation.

When you have started work on the piece, try to devise a section at a time and make sure that other dancers watch your work, even if it is only a minute's worth of choreography at a time. You can build on this. If you have a group of dancers, let some work on one section while others work on a different section. Always share your work towards the end of each session so that every member of the group feels happy about what has been devised and can learn it if necessary.

Staging

A bare set with few props is one of Bruce's fingerprints. Use props in your piece, but rather than using a chair or another prop from one of Bruce's pieces, find some of your own that are appropriate for your piece.

Use a simplistic set and use lighting that enhances the action, creates mood or has symbolic meaning. You may wish to have realistic costume, but remember that costume is also used by Bruce to reflect character and status.

Find your own music or even compose some yourself, rather than using the music from any of Bruce's works. If you are basing your piece on a study of *Swansong*, try to find or create instrumental music and use sound effects. Remember to use silence as well as sounds that you can make with your body or other objects. Compose or find different music for different sections and mix this with silence.

Performing repertoire by Newson

Here you can choose to perform a solo or a group piece. Remember that each candidate needs three minutes' exposure, so when choosing an extract to perform, you will need to look carefully at the length of the extract, and where you might cut it so as to make it intelligible to an audience.

> **Think about...**
> Check your health and safety before embarking on working in a Newson way. The work is very physical and risks are taken.

Setting your stage

In Newson's work, the stage is often elaborate in design and would be extremely difficult to reproduce. Choose an extract therefore that is set in a fairly neutral environment, and that is not dependent on a set that you cannot hope to reproduce.

Music and sound

In terms of sound, you might wish to use background noises that have been previously recorded – people talking in a pub, for example. The extract might be performed in silence. There might be some spoken dialogue, or music to accompany the performance. Pay careful attention to the details of the soundtrack on the video of the piece studied and decide how to reproduce them.

Costume

Examine what is worn by the performers on the video of the piece and find something that represents the same status. In *Strange Fish* the costumes are everyday wear from the 1980s, but they are not elaborate. Remember that you need to be able to perform in them and they must feel comfortable. If you wear a short dress, then wear shorts underneath. You might need to use props, such as blonde wigs. If you use a pint glass for *Enter Achilles*, make sure that it is plastic – do not use real glass on stage.

Taking risks

DV8's work is highly physical and often dangerous. Make sure that your performance space is safe for you and your audience. If you need safety mats then use them. Discuss the choice of extract with your teacher and take all necessary safety precautions. Wear knee and elbow pads to protect your body. Check with the teacher and the technician that you are following health and safety regulations when using things like water on stage. Ask your teacher to fill in a risk assessment form.

Devising in the style of Newson

The option to devise in the style of Newson is generally more popular than performing a piece of Newson's repertoire. Look again at the fingerprints of Newson's work and the type of themes that emerge from it. Look at the subject matter and his treatment of taboo subjects. You do not need to find wide topics. Find something that you yourself have experienced or witnessed.

Subject matter

 Consider, for example, the concept of competition between friends of the same gender, or the difference in behaviour of a group of females when a) males are absent and b) males are present. Observe the differences in behaviour, discuss them with your group and make a list of them. You might go on to discuss flirtation and the variety of techniques people employ: fluttering eyelashes, playing with hair, leaning forward and so on. You could try some short improvisations based on these ideas and record them on video. Watch each other improvise, give constructive feedback and work on exaggerating particular movements, gestures and facial expressions. Use repetition of movements and experiment with building up tension to a climax point.

Try also an improvisation where you annoy each other. Conversely, try to please each other, and establish honest relationships within the group.

Newson's work is about relationships between people and how they develop. It examines behaviour between people of the same gender and then between men and women. He does not conform to stereotypes. There is a strong element of inventing a new movement language for each piece. Your movement language will depend on the subject matter of your devised piece.

Structure

Once you have the subject matter in place, work out the length of the piece you need to ensure equal exposure for everyone in the group. Decide how many sections are needed and the various relationships between the dancers: solos, duets, trios, quartets, ensembles and so on. Allow dancers to work on separate sections and then bring them together to share the work created so far. This helps speed up the process in the early stages. Remember that if a student is working on a solo, other students in the group can suggest movements, pathways, gestures and so on. Take turns in directing each other and keep working as a unit.

The beginning of the piece should intrigue the audience. There should be at least one climatic point. The pace could start slow and build up through the use of repetition and exaggeration to become fast before a climax. Silence and stasis are used to effect. The ending of a Newson piece is often left open to interpretation and challenges the audience.

Taking risks

The set is integral to Newson's work. Obviously you do not have access to the funds he has, but you do need to use your performance space in a challenging way. Look at how you can use the walls and the audience area – do not be scared to make your audience move position. Newson has used bathtubs, water under floorboards, beds, a rolling hill, boxes and a pub to name but a few unusual sets and props. You can find cheap alternatives such as cardboard boxes to reconstruct sets. You could perform in an unusual place, such as a children's playground. Whatever you decide to do, talk it through with your teacher and ensure that it is safe. Although Newson's work is about breaking boundaries, health and safety for all concerned must be uppermost in your minds at all times.

Rehearsing and performing

Once you have devised your piece, you need to rehearse it as much as possible to make sure that it is as good as it can be for the performance. Don't keep rehearsing a section that you enjoy performing, however tempting this may be. Work on the weaker sections and perfect them. Always rehearse the ending and the bows. Try to perform the work right through from beginning to end as often as possible, even if there are parts that you're not happy with.

Work in front of a mirror some of the time, but always rehearse in the space in which you will perform the piece for the examination. Video your work in rehearsal and watch it back.

Make your costumes early on and dance in them so that on the day of the **dress rehearsal** you are used to performing in them. Look after them carefully and make sure you each have your own labelled bag or hanger in which to keep them. Try out any make-up you are going to wear for the exam and make sure that it does not come off on your clothes.

Tip

If you have a black floor and a black backcloth, don't wear a black costume as the video will not show you clearly.

When it comes to the final performance of your devised piece, reread the advice given above on performing your repertoire piece.

Drama

When you first approach a drama text, you need to decide what the main subject or issue is that needs to be communicated to the audience. Think about how you will convey your understanding of the play and why you want to do so. Remember that your performance should demonstrate the typical traits or fingerprints of the practitioner, so don't be too creative in your interpretation.

There are obvious considerations when choosing your extract, such as the number of performers in your group and the gender of these performers. You have to consider the time constraints, of course, and decide what you can feasibly perform in the time required for your group's size. You may wish to take a continuous section from the play. This may stand on its own, or you may wish to represent the action of before and after in some way. You could choose one aspect of the play as a focus and then cut it down so that you only perform the parts that relate to this aspect.

Once you have decided on your extract, you need to work on physicalising and vocalising the text.

Work on the volume of your voice. Make sure you can project it adequately. Be very careful about pace and diction. Make sure that you don't rush through your lines: don't just say them, perform them. Practise speaking the words and make sure that your

Physicalising and vocalising

pronunciation is good and the words are clearly understood. This may sound obvious, but on the day of the performance you will probably be nervous and you need to be well rehearsed in the delivery of your lines to ensure that the examiner understands everything you say.

The role you play may suggest a certain tone of voice or accent. It is very important that you practise this if it is different from your own usual tone or accent. Putting on an accent can be very difficult and is something to be avoided unless you're sure you can pull it off.

When you think about physicalising the text, return to the drama section in the Language of Performing Arts section and remind yourself of the techniques discussed there. How would your character move? What do you want your body language to convey? Be careful about the use of mime – it's all too easy to pick up an imaginary object and then forget you are holding it! If you are going to have imaginary props then make sure you are well rehearsed in using them.

Look at any stage directions specified by the playwright, as well as any clues about the pace and tension of the extract you're performing. Think about how you can use blocking and levels to good effect.

Performing repertoire by Brecht

The episodic nature of Brecht's work, and the fact that it doesn't adhere to dramatic unities, means that it is relatively easy to find scenes that stand on their own without having to worry about filling in the before and after. If you want to 'set the scene', you could use the very Brechtian device of a narrator to do so, as well as to comment on the action.

Look carefully at how Brecht creates tension in the scenes you're performing. What sort of pace should there be? Does this change? Remember that you need to build tension and make the piece dramatic without becoming lost in the emotion or letting the audience become lost in the emotion.

Your performance space should appear to be exactly that: a performance space. There should be no attempt to create the illusion of another setting. You should have simple white lighting and the areas of the stage and theatre space should be exposed for the audience to see. Any costume changes should be made in full view of the audience.

Put a costume rail on stage so performers can fetch their costumes from it. Rehearse changing costume. It should be fast and slick. Costumes and props can be left at appropriate positions on the stage, but do not make it difficult for yourselves. Use the set to make life easier in this regard: use a block to create a table, and put a hat on it so that you can put it on easily for a quick but noticeable change of character.

Work on Gestus. Consider how your character relates to the others in the play; consider what their social role is and how this could be conveyed through stylised movements, manner, facial expressions and so on. In order to distance the audience from the characters, you could consider swapping roles during the piece.

Let's look at *The Caucasian Chalk Circle* as an example. There are many suitable monologues, **duologues** and ensemble opportunities in this text. If you wished to perform a monologue, you could perform Azdak's speech in Scene 5, where he teaches the Grand Duke to eat like a poor person. Another monologue opportunity could be Grusha's deliberations about taking the baby at the end of Scene 2: you would have to deliver the narrator's lines as well, but this is perfectly acceptable. Consider using lighting effects to show the passing of time: lights fading to darkness and then fading up again to represent morning, for example.

Duologues can be taken from the conversations between Simon and Grusha or the two Ironshirts. Make sure that each actor has equal exposure and that the pieces do not overrun. The examiner keeps a close eye on their watch and can stop you if the piece is too long. Scene 6 'The Chalk Circle' is ideal as a group scene, as actors can multi-role to make up exposure time. Equally, 'Crossing the Bridge' offers opportunities for a more physical interpretation.

More than one person can play the role of Grusha (or another central character) if the extract chosen is quite long and the group is large. A simple shawl could be used to denote the character of Grusha, and can be swapped from actor to actor as appropriate.

If there is an opportunity to use music and song, you should make sure you do so. At first, the Narrator's singing will probably have seemed strange to you. You don't have to use his musical style, but make sure that the words can be understood by the audience. Unaccompanied singing is acceptable, but if you can make your performance more interesting by using instruments, then do so. The scene with the marriage to the dying man is humorous, although poignant for Grusha. Music and song have a ceremonial role to play here.

Devising in the style of Brecht

What do you want your devised piece to be about: what social issues are important to you? What do you want your audience to learn from your work? Think about how you can make your piece didactic, so that it conveys a message to the audience and makes them go away and think about what you have presented to them and why.

Clearly, one of the most obvious ways in which you can make your piece Brechtian is to make use of the Verfremdungseffekt. As discussed in the chapter on Contextual Studies, there are several ways in which you can make sure your audience is constantly aware that they are watching actors perform a play, and therefore that they do not become emotionally engaged in the action, but intellectually engaged in the issues behind the action.

You could introduce your piece, perhaps with a narrator, or with placards or projections. You could make use of these during the piece as well, to signal to your audience what you want them to be thinking about as they watch you perform.

Caucasian Chalk Circle

> **Tip**
> If you are delivering a monologue, you are allowed other performers on stage so you have a focus point to work around, but they must not deliver any lines.

Verfremdungseffekt

Structure

You could break up the dramatic unities, by jumping backwards and forwards in time, by changing locations, or by following more than one story line, though don't try to make the piece too complicated for the short performance time that you have. You could devise your piece so that it is made up of a montage of episodes or scenes, and make the structure obvious to the audience by breaking it up with poems or songs that emphasise the point your piece is making. Keep in mind through all of this, however, that you are still presenting a piece that should be dramatic. You want to avoid simplistic and transparent emotional triggers, but your piece will need tension and drama to have the necessary impact.

Language

Consider what kind of language you want to use. You may wish to include songs and poetry and mix these in with formal dialogue. Remember that Brecht's work is often intended to create humour to convey its serious subject matter. How could you incorporate humour into your piece?

Types

Are your characters going to be named or representational types? Or a mixture of the two? Using names that simply represent a type, such as The Cook or The Teacher will help to distance your audience and avoid them becoming too involved, since it is harder to get caught up in the story of a type than a fully rounded character. The character types are intended to represent a point of view rather than a person.

Performing repertoire by Godber

When you come to performing a piece of Godber's work, there are various elements of the drama that you need to work on to ensure that you give a convincing performance, and to make sure that you bring out Godber's fingerprints in the extract you perform.

A play such as *Bouncers* is made up of many short episodes and it should not therefore be too difficult to choose an extract or extracts that stand alone. If you choose to perform a play by Godber that involves multi-roles, you will have to work hard at the techniques required to make it effective. It is not at all easy to switch rapidly from one role into another, very different, part, and it will require a great deal of practice and rehearsal.

> "Wherever you are in the world, if you're with a group of more than ten male actors, it's a fair bet that two of them will have been in a production of *Bouncers*."
>
> Dominic Dromgoole, *The Full Room* (Methuen 2000)

Structure

Once you've chosen which extract of the play you're going to perform, explore the phrasing and sequencing of the text. You may wish to map the scene or scenes so that you can mark out the dynamics, the shape and build of the piece. Look carefully at the stage directions and see if they indicate how the scenes build. For example, in *Bouncers*, the sudden blackout and change of pace as the bouncers establish themselves only works if the sequence of scenes building up to this break has been 'fast and hectic' as the stage directions indicate. Furthermore, you must ensure that the transitions between short scenes are as tight as the dialogue and action in the scenes themselves.

Structure wheel

Construct a structure wheel, using different colours to show rising and falling levels of tension and climax. See page 53.

Timing

Much of the audience enjoyment of Godber's work relies heavily on timing for jokes, effects and the choral moments. Get the timing wrong and it looks very wooden and like a first reading. Just because there is a keen sense of pace to the work, does not mean you have to rush it.

For example, in *Bouncers*, look at the moment when Judd turns from the barber into Terry. After Judd's line 'I'm here' there's a beat, before the others turn to the audience and say 'I thought he was the barber'. That beat allows thinking time for the switch between actor and character, and provides the set-up for an audience laugh. If that beat is too long, the audience will still understand, but the laugh will get lost. If it's too short, the audience won't have enough of their own thinking time to follow and will miss everything. *Bouncers* is only a short play, but you need to work in as detailed a way as possible to ensure that your timing is immaculate. You will soon know if you've got it right, since, as well as all the other antics you might get up to, the audience will laugh at the timing.

There are only four performers in *Bouncers*, and they work as a number of characters. One of the biggest challenges is to ensure that there is a complementary variety in the way in which they are presented. Your scenes need to be carefully blocked to avoid everything ending up in a line. Use the depth of the available space so that items or moments can be placed in the foreground while the next is already being set up behind it and can take the focus away, through being upstage, at the moment you want to switch the focus. The same idea can be applied to shifting the focus of the action from one side of the stage to the other.

Proxemics

The sequence in which the boys Terry, Jerry, Kev and Baz line up in front of the stage to do their pre-night checks is probably the only time there should be a line.

Keep the use of space as tight as the timing. The original production played on a very shallow stage in front of a curtain with two beer kegs as the text suggests. You can maximise the physical aspects of the acting by having your backs turned away from the audience, in the hot-dog stand scene for example.

Dialogue

You will find that you learn the lines more easily through rehearsal with action rather than learning by rote. However, learning the lines is only the first part of the process. You then need to polish the dialogue.

Look out for short one-line phrases, comments that are batted between the characters. This should work just like a tennis match: there's a rally back and forth and the point is won with a convincing shot:

JUDD   Burn her face off

LES   Oh, don't be daft, Elaine.

ERIC   Castrate the philanderer.

RALPH   Finish with him.

Choral speech requires you to think about having similar intonation, emphasis, pause and pace in even the simplest of lines:

ALL   Scenes from Dante's Inferno!

Start with short lines like this and be willing to listen to each other so that you can adjust your speech to theirs. Decide for yourselves what you want to achieve from speaking together.

" The thing about theatre, if it works, is that it makes you feel – society desensitises the human soul, art and theatre re-sensitises you and makes you feel uncomfortable. "

Godber, Talkback at the Hull Truck Theatre, 2001.

One of the simple rules of comedy, known as the rule of three, is: set-up – development – punchline. For example,

ERIC   Oooooooh, it goes right through me.

RALPH   It goes right through me an' all.

LES   What hasn't?

The trick is not to alert the audience ahead of time. If they think they are being cued up for a joke they will tend to work against it. Comedy requires you to engage in a complex relationship with the audience – don't shy away from it, but always stay in control, even if at times you let the audience think they are in charge.

Action

While the action and activity in Godber's plays is just as important as the words, that does not mean that everyone has to be running around frenetically just to create a sense of pace in the piece.

> The *Thriller* video should be carefully studied in order to achieve just the right elements of parody.

The stage directions for the *Thriller* video give you a strong message about the way in which movement in the whole play should be approached. In other words, it is not good enough to do a sloppy reference to the *Thriller* dance from the video – it needs to be studied to create what Godber calls 'a complicated rip-off'.

So, ensure that when you create a walk for one of the characters, it is replicated or amplified each time the character appears.

Exploit the physical theatre aspects of this style. The beer kegs, for example, aren't just there to provide appropriate looking stools. They could be used to illustrate Lucky Eric's power-lifting, or the dryer in the hairdresser's.

Try to remember that not all drunks act in the same way. The range of drunks in *Bouncers* represents varying degrees of aggression and stupor. You need to make that variety come to life: this need not be from personal experience! Use observations from people you know, your relatives at family gatherings or people you may have seen on the street at pub closing time. Unless the characters behave in a recognisable way, they won't get the laughs.

> 66 I think modern theatre audiences are quite sophisticated; they watch lots of videos, they watch films, they watch telly, they watch adverts – information comes very, very quickly. In the theatre we have to be aware of that, we have to be aware that brevity is the soul of wit... just say it and get on with it; the audience will come with you. 99
>
> Godber, Talkback at the Hull Truck Theatre, 2001.

Finally, you need to study some actual bouncers. It's not advisable to do this at too close a range and certainly don't try asking a group of club doormen if you can study them for the evening! It might be a good idea to improvise in your drama studio around what you've observed to build the characters of Judd or Les, but it is not advisable on a busy Friday night!

Devising in the style of Godber

Some people are dismissive about Godber's standing in the pantheon of playwrights, but don't be deceived by what appears to be a basic formulaic style. If you manage to do justice to it, then you will know how much hard work it can be to develop and deliver.

Here are some suggestions that you might wish to consider when devising in the style of Godber. Consider also the comments made under repertoire *above*.

Regional elements

Godber's plays have a particular regional outlook, based in the north of England, though their appeal extends well beyond this. Try to think of something that is locally recognisable, but also likely to be more universally understood. Use local expressions and references to colour the work. Use what you know. You will find that being honest with yourselves will result in far more fun both for your group and for the audience.

Traffic wardens, supermarket checkout assistants or tourism industry workers in Newquay could all offer ample material for a 20-minute piece that exploits this style. Single gender groups can be useful when it comes to taking stereotypes from the opposite sex, but you do not need to use four men or four women as Godber did in *Bouncers* and *Shakers*. In *Teechers*, three actors are expected to play a multitude of mixed-gender roles.

Coarse language is typical of Godber's plays. However, beware of using much swearing when devising your dialogue. It may appear that you've put it in arbitrarily rather than for its dramatic or comic effect, and it may prove distracting for you as performers and for the audience. Explore how you can play with the words to create the same effect and laughs. Godber uses the colloquial 'Chuffin' hell!', for example. Try inventing your own expletives that relate to the theme.

What observations are you aiming to make about society or the world in your piece? You will recall that Godber decided that writing for soaps was limiting and that unless he was 'opening a vein with the writing' then there was little point in doing it. So, try to find the social comment you wish to make. Remember, it is a careful balance that needs to be struck; otherwise you will have the audience laughing at things that you are concerned about, or uncomfortable because they are embarrassed by your treatment of an issue. The key is not to start with the issues, let them emerge as the piece develops. Develop the character types, and then the characters within that type, next the situations, and then the issue.

Consider how Godber evokes a mixed reaction to his characters, despite their obvious 'types'. For example, the audience laughs at the antics of the bouncers, at their expressions, at their lampoons of the people with whom they interact, but no one wants to take them home for the evening. We might empathise with 'the wise old owl' Lucky Eric's concern for the way young women are treated and treat themselves, but we are left appalled by the way he enjoys the softness of the cracking heads. We laugh when Ralph offers the still-warm basket meal he's found, but we are disgusted to realise that it's quite likely that one of them might actually want to eat it.

Music

Whether you are performing repertoire by Gershwin or Reich, you need to assess your own musical skills and experience. There is one absolutely fundamental question you need to answer honestly before you decide to perform any song by George Gershwin or anyone else: can you sing in tune? If you cannot sing in tune – or keep in tune after practice – then whatever else you do with the songs is likely to go unnoticed. If keeping in tune is a problem but you play an instrument, you could play an instrumental version. With pieces by Steve Reich, some of them will require that you

Opening the vein

See pages 79 and 81–82.

> " What we can't do is bore the audience. If you start to bore the audience you start to get indulgent, and as we get better and better and better and we stretch the audience emotionally we have to be more workman-like in taking the audience on different kinds of journeys. "
>
> Godber, Talkback at the Hull Truck Theatre, 2001.

play an instrument, but there are some that you can perform if you don't already have experience of playing a musical instrument. See page 133 for suggestions of Reich pieces.

Performing repertoire by Gershwin

When choosing which of Gershwin's songs to perform, you need to assess honestly how capable you are at singing. Some songs are more chromatic than others and are therefore potentially more challenging. It may be that you can hold a straightforward melody but struggle with chromatic melodies, in which case you would be better to avoid *It ain't necessarily so* and *They can't take that away from me*.

If holding a melody is no problem for you, you have the complete range of Gershwin's songs to choose from, but there are various points to consider when looking at the possibilities.

Do I want to perform on my own or with others?

With Gershwin's songs, it's tempting to want to do a solo since so many famous performances of his works are by solo artists, but it's easier to make a performance out of the songs if you work on them as a group. It's perfectly all right for you (or other members of the group) to play instruments. In fact, you do not have to sing at all – you could decide to produce an instrumental version of the songs you select.

If you decide to perform with others and you all want to sing, you must **not** all sing in unison since this will almost certainly mean that the examiner will not be able to distinguish between you. You either need to sing different songs in a **medley** or work out harmonies for everyone to sing while each person in turn has the opportunity to sing a song of their choice. A good number of people for a medley would be four, as you could then perform the four songs that you have studied and show how creative you can be in linking them together.

Once you have decided on your songs, there are a number of elements to consider in order to make your performance as good as it can be.

Pitch
We have already mentioned the importance of keeping in tune and to do this you need to be completely confident about the melody of the song and be able to pitch every entry. Most of Gershwin's songs have one or two phrases that are quite awkward to pitch and you need to be able to hear these in your head without having to rely on the piano or other accompaniment.

Timing
If you are nervous you may be tempted to rush your singing and this will mean that the emotional content of the songs will be lost. A successful performance of songs in this style means understanding the best tempo at which to perform the songs. You may find that you have a number of recordings of a song, all at different tempos. This need not be confusing – use it as an opportunity to make a creative decision as to which is the most effective speed for that song.

Diction
Sloppy diction will undermine the wit and sparkle of what you are singing. As we have seen in the discussion on Contextual Studies,

Remember that if you're performing repertoire, you must perform one or more of the songs that you have studied for the Contextual Studies written examination paper.

Tip

Get one or more recordings of the song(s) you intend to sing and learn them off by heart. Learn the words from the sheet music rather than the CD to make sure you have the correct version.

Ira Gershwin's lyrics are very similar to the style of Gilbert and Sullivan's work – fast, slick and witty. You need to get your tongue around these words and **articulate** every single syllable clearly.

In particular, make sure that you do **not** pronounce 'th' as 'f' or the word 'with' as 'wiv'. You can introduce a slight American accent to the songs if you wish but do not colour the singing with UK accents, irrespective of where you come from. If you have a tongue stud – take it out! It is almost impossible to sing these songs unless your tongue is completely free.

It's easy to forget to breathe when you're nervous. There are all sorts of techniques for breathing effectively and using breath control to relax yourself during the performance. Think back to the work you did in the Language of Performing Arts unit. Appearing confident and relaxed is a performance technique you can use if you learn how to breathe properly and control your intake and exhalation effectively.

Gershwin's songs need to feel alive. They are witty, stylish and emotional, and you need to communicate this to your audience. You can do this by varying such elements as volume, pacing and intensity but no one will think your performance is the real thing unless you can communicate through your face as well. You need to look enthusiastic in your performance so that your audience feels that you are actually singing these words to *them*.

No one wants to watch a singer who looks awkward, slouches or fiddles while singing. Make a video recording of yourself so that you can see what you look like when you're performing. This can be a rather harsh experience, but it's one of the most effective ways to see what the audience is seeing and think how you would react if you were presented with yourself singing.

Use your space to its best effect. Don't perform in a cramped space as it will make you feel constrained. Most music rooms are completely unsuitable places to perform in, as they have lots of equipment scattered around the room, have little flexibility and restricted space to house an audience. See whether you can use the same space you will be using for the dance and drama performances, but remember that you need to choose somewhere with good **acoustics** – the curtains or drapes in drama studios can deaden the sound.

You need to 'set' the songs. Gershwin's songs offer huge possibilities for you to make a real performance event out of them. George and Ira Gershwin were part of the fashionable high society of the 1920s and 1930s in New York and then Hollywood. Your performance needs to reflect that, so the more razzamatazz you can inject into it, the stronger the similarities will be. For the examination you could dress in formal evening wear, set out the room in cabaret style and use appropriate lighting.

Finally, if you're performing with others, you need to make the ensemble work for everyone. There's no room for any passengers in the group: everyone needs to play their role. In particular if you are all singing, work out the best use of space for everyone. Arrange the

Tip

Try using a tongue-twister to warm up in rehearsals, for example the opening lyrics from *Nice Work*: 'The man who only lives for making money lives a life that isn't necessarily funny.'

Breath control

Facial expression

Tip

Eyes and teeth are the crucial elements in singing a Gershwin song – you need to smile with both your eyes and your teeth!

Posture

Use of space

Tip

Your performance needs to be authentic – standing in a cluttered music room singing along with a piano, dressed in jeans, T-shirt and trainers is very unlikely to produce an appropriate atmosphere.

Working as a group

Gershwin's 'fingerprints'

Remember that, since the lyrics were added later, the thematic content of the songs is not a 'fingerprint' of George Gershwin's style.

Selecting a chord structure

Experimenting with melody

Deciding on a structure

ensemble so that there is good eye contact between everyone – and don't be afraid to smile at each other!

Devising in the style of Gershwin

The points that we've just made about performing a piece by Gershwin will apply equally if you devise a piece in Gershwin's style yourself. It's important, therefore, to make sure that whatever material you decide to include in your piece, it must have scope for you to perform it in the same way as a piece that Gershwin wrote.

Let's remind ourselves of three of the most important fingerprints of George Gershwin's style.

➢ Strong **harmonic progressions**

➢ Memorable melodies and witty lyrics

➢ Clear structure to the song with each section worked out effectively.

Gershwin tends to use these features in each of his songs. They are all intertwined, but we will look at a way in which you can mould them into an original song in the style of Gershwin.

If you select the type of chord sequence that Gershwin would have used, it will be so much easier to make the rest of the song sound authentic. You could use a progression from an existing song – after all, the chord progressions are often not unique to Gershwin. Here is a sequence of eight chords you could experiment with – it's very similar to the opening of *They all laughed*. It's in the key of C major and each chord lasts for two beats.

C	A minor	D minor	G	D minor	G	C	G7

You'll need to record this onto a sequencer, experiment with it on the keyboard or ask someone else to play it through. You could use this two or three times as the basis of the first section of the song. Don't be afraid to adapt the chord structure for the third or fourth line and you obviously need to finish the section with a chord of C major lasting four beats or more to make it sound finished.

Now take the phrase and experiment with improvising a tune over the top. Don't worry about words at this stage – we'll add those later, just as the Gershwins did. Simply hum or sing to 'la' over the chords until you have a snippet of melody that you like. Repeat this until you have built up three or four phrases for the first section. You could try using a pentatonic melody as Gershwin's songs are full of these.

All you then have to do is to decide on the overall structure. Once you've finished the first section, you could decide to compose the song in ternary form so that the last section will be more or less the same as the one you've just written. You then need to compose a contrasting middle section using a different chord progression. Or you could decide to simply write a verse and chorus. If you choose to do this then what you did first might be the chorus, especially if it's quite fast and has a catchy melody. You would then need to produce a short verse to go before it.

In some ways, the lyrics are the least important aspect of the song. You just need to make sure that you choose some words that fit the rhythm of the music exactly. They need to rhyme and the overall verse or chorus has to make sense. It doesn't matter if you think the words sound a bit cheesy – most of Gershwin's songs would be unlikely to stand the test of time as poetry. Think about witty rhymes you could use and be as inventive as possible.

Performing repertoire by Reich

You need to think carefully when choosing a piece by Steve Reich to perform. We've spent some time looking at *Different Trains* in the previous chapter, but you would only be able to perform this piece if you play in a string quartet. There are a number of Steve Reich's pieces that would be suitable for repertoire performance, though, and it's probably useful for you (and your teachers) to think about the following list.

All of these pieces were written in Reich's early period between 1967 and 1973. In this period, Reich's music was obviously minimalist because it uses very simple ideas that repeat over and over again. These ideas are used to build up the structure of the piece.

Piece	Performers	Date
Piano Phase	Two piano players	1967
Violin Phase	One or more violinists	1967
Four Organs	Up to four keyboard players	1970
Clapping Music	Two performers	1972
Music for Pieces of Wood	Five pairs of tuned claves	1973

To perform *Piano Phase* or *Violin Phase* you would need to be able to play either the piano or violin. However, you would be able to put together a performance of *Four Organs*, *Clapping Music* or *Music for Pieces of Wood* even if you had not played an instrument before. The most important skill in these pieces is to be able to count and keep in time with the other performers.

Performing a piece by Steve Reich is a little different from performing a song by Gershwin (or any other songwriter). This is partly because in a song, one of the main purposes of the performance is to communicate the meaning of the song to an audience. Reich's music is not intended to communicate in the same way – the emotion comes from the audience being drawn into the power and energy of the rhythms of the piece.

Bearing that in mind, here are some of the most important things you need to remember when performing Reich's music. Before you start, get a recording of the piece you are going to perform and listen to it until you are completely familiar with every aspect of the piece. If you are performing an extract of the piece, you still need to be aware of which part of the piece you are performing.

One of the features of many of Reich's pieces is that they are performed by his own group of performers, Steve Reich and

Producing lyrics

Tip

Remember that you don't have to perform the whole piece. Everyone in the group needs to have three minutes of exposure but as all of Reich's pieces are ensemble pieces, all the performers have constant exposure. You will need to decide how much to perform.

Ensemble arrangement

Further reading

Reich's *Writings on Music 1965–2000* (Oxford University Press 2002).

Musicians. In some of his scores, Reich has diagrams of how the performers should be positioned in relation to each other. For example, in *Four Organs*, Reich has the performers sitting in a semicircle with the maracas player in the centre so that they can all see one another. It's best if you don't double any of the parts – each person should have something different to do at any one point of the piece.

Posture

Posture is equally important. Reich's performers are often static – in other words, there is hardly any movement. In a performance of *Music for Pieces of Wood*, for example, the performers often stand in a semicircle with very little lower body movement. Of course, if you're playing the wooden claves you will need some upper body movement to make sure that the sounds echo as you hit the claves.

Keeping in time

Obviously, since Reich is a percussionist, the rhythmic aspects of these pieces are absolutely central. If your performance is not in time with the other members of the group you will not be very successful. The tempo of most of the pieces is very fast, however, so you'll need to practise slowly and speed up as you become more proficient. It would be best to use a metronome to help you keep in time. We suggest that you practise short sections at a slow tempo and then speed up a little at a time until you can perform the piece at the same tempo as the recording. Don't worry if you can't go as fast as the recording, though. It's more important to perform accurately and precisely.

Energy

Whatever tempo you choose for your final performance, you'll have to make sure that the energy level is high. You can still show a high level of energy even if the piece is not that fast. Make sure that every note you play has plenty of attack and that you clap, hit the claves or play the note on an instrument with confidence and determination.

Focus

You need to concentrate to play this sort of music. Wandering eyes, sloppy posture, flicking hair, shuffling or any other distractions are completely inappropriate. In fact, anything that might distract the audience visually is to be avoided in Reich. We've said it a few times already, but it's worth saying again, performing a piece by Reich is not the same as singing a song by Gershwin.

Music technology

In Reich's later pieces he makes use of music technology, mainly to provide speech samples that are part of the music, but you could do the same thing with repertoire performances. You could record one or more tracks onto a computer sequencing package or a multi-track tape recorder and then play along with the tape. This is what is intended in the case of *Violin Phase* although it can also be performed as an ensemble with other performers.

Devising in the style of Reich

The points that we've just made about performing a piece by Reich will apply equally if you devise a piece in Reich's style yourself. It's important, therefore, to make sure that whatever material you decide to include in your piece, it has scope for you to perform it in the same way as a piece that Reich wrote.

Reich's fingerprints

Remind yourself of some of the fingerprints of Steve Reich's style and then decide which ones you want to use, for example:

➢ Short rhythmic or melodic units that intertwine

➢ Rapid tempos

➢ Phasing/counterpoint

➢ Speech extracts.

You need to remember that Steve Reich does not normally use all of these ideas in every piece – and neither should you! You need to work within some aspects of his style rather than trying to use every aspect. For example, not all of his pieces use speech extracts so you don't have to use that particular aspect if you don't want to. However, some features are more important than others. Simply writing a piece in a rapid tempo is no guarantee that it will sound like a piece by Reich. It's the way that Reich combines these elements that makes his style unique.

Here are some ideas about how you can build up a piece.

You need to devise a short rhythm or melody first of all. It's a good idea to keep this within eight beats, as Reich's musical phrases are usually short. Decide how fast you want the tempo to be: Reich's tempos are normally very fast. Why not set the metronome to a fast speed such as 160 – this can act as the pulse of the piece.

You could use a pentatonic melody, using only the black notes on the piano; this would probably sound a little like the style of Reich's melodic ideas. Experiment with a few ideas. Make sure that you don't just have one note per beat, as Reich's motifs are never that slow. Try to get two notes on every tick of the metronome. It should start to sound a little like Reich as you repeat it over and over again.

You can record this idea on the computer sequencer when you're happy with it. Then try phase-shifting the unit. If there are three or four of you, each try shifting the phase and experiment with what happens. Remember to keep the energy level high and don't vary the volume. As with Reich's pieces, you need to practise until you can play the units at a fast tempo.

You might not want to use an exact phase shift. In Reich's later works, he uses counterpoint but not in such an exact way as he used the earlier technique of phasing. Depending on how you work out the original unit, you could make a second part fit over the top.

Reich creates music in some pieces by using extracts from speech. But you need to be careful how you choose the extracts. For Reich, there were some strict criteria. These were:

➢ It had to be short – normally lasting only a couple of seconds.

➢ It had to be musically interesting – a particular accent or way of saying certain words.

➢ The phrase had to have a 'natural' melodic shape so when you heard it over and over again it began to sound like a melody.

➢ The speech extract had to have a natural rhythm.

➢ It was always recorded – never performed live.

So you can't just sit with a microphone speaking words in your performance. You need to select speech extracts using the above

Short rhythmic or melodic units

Tip

It's important that your rhythmic motifs carry on continuously. Don't use a long note at the end of the motif or it will sound as if the music is always stopping. You want the motif to repeat seamlessly as in *Piano Phase* or *Clapping Music*.

Phasing or counterpoint

Speech extracts

criteria, record them and then weave them into a piece of music so that one or more instruments copy the same notes as the speaker's voice.

You need to have a theme to your speech samples. This could be autobiographical, or it might be based on a topical issue that you or your group feel strongly about. Whatever theme you choose, you need to compile a good selection of speech samples as you may not use all of them. When you record your speech samples there are a few things to remember:

➢ Aim to record between six and 12 speech samples

➢ Make sure that you get a good range of female and male speakers so that your composition has an interesting texture

➢ Keep the samples short – many of those used by Reich consist of only a few words

➢ Keep a catalogue of who the speakers are so that you can construct your piece around the use of the voices

➢ Try to transcribe your speech samples into musical notation.

It is preferable to record your speech extracts digitally (for example, on minidisk or sampling keyboard) as this will enable you to incorporate your recordings into your composition if you use music technology. However, it is perfectly possible to use a tape recorder as a basis for your recordings as long as the quality is good enough.

Reich allowed the patterns of the speech samples to dictate the pitch shape and rhythm of the melodies that accompany them. As soon as you have catalogued each of your speech samples, you need to choose an instrumental timbre to accompany each one – Reich used a string quartet in his composition to create an interesting and varied texture. You may wish to perform live in this way or alternatively to use synthesised sounds from electronic equipment. For example, you might use a cello sound to double a medium or high male voice, whereas you might select a violin or flute sound to double a mid-to-high female voice. You do not have to use the same instrumental sound to double the same speech sample all of the way through – in fact, you might want to colour a particular speech sample by using two or three different sounds to represent changes in mood or a change of section within the structure.

Phasing or counterpoint

You might want to use some phasing techniques in your piece. In that way, you could show that you understand the way in which Reich used speech in the past. On the other hand, if you are able to sample the speech extracts, it may be more interesting for you to position these extracts within the overall piece.

Structure

Make a diagram to represent the structure of the piece that you intend to compose – you can always modify this as your work develops. You will need to ask yourself the following questions:

➢ How long will the piece last?

➢ How many movements or sections will there be?

➢ How will the speech samples be allocated to each section?

Tip

If no one in your group is able to transcribe speech samples you could ask your teacher to help. There are no marks for doing it but it will help you to talk about it to the visiting examiner before the performance.

Remember that each member of the group needs to have three minutes of exposure during the piece.

➤ Will they tell a story or simply provide a commentary on an issue or situation?

Using sounds

You might want to use sampled sounds as well as speech. Reich does this in *City Life* and these sounds can add a new dimension to the piece as a whole. If you decide to do this, you'll need to make sure that the sounds are related to the 'story' of the piece. Just having additional sounds for the sake of it makes the piece feel as though it is full of sound effects and may create a different impression from what you want.

When you have assembled the structure, it is as important to rehearse a devised piece as an extract, so be disciplined and plan a rehearsal schedule.

A final word

Whatever art form or practitioner you use, enjoy your performance and try to ensure that your audience – and the examiner – enjoys it as well.

Glossary

Accompaniment. In music, the part that supports the melody and that tends to be played by deeper-sounding instruments or the left hand of the piano. *See also* **melody**.

Acoustics. The structural properties of a performance space that allow it to transmit, enhance or deaden the sound of a performer's voice or instrument.

Action. 1. In dance, the motions used. 2. In drama, the content of a piece as played out by the actors.

Allegory. A story that works on two or more levels: the literal meaning and the deeper symbolic meaning that the audience is meant to pick up on.

Allusion. A reference made to something by hinting at it rather than mentioning it directly or explicitly.

Analogy. A comparison between a complex or unfamiliar idea and one that is more straightforward or well known, using the simpler example to make the more complex issue clearer or easier to imagine. The two need not be similar except in the specific point of comparison. For example, imagining the expansion of the universe in terms of the expansion of a balloon being inflated.

Animate. Literally, to bring to life. The act of dramatising a story is sometimes referred to as 'animating the story'. This is distinct from cartoon animations.

Aphorism. A short saying that contains a statement of truth or principle, for example 'Lost time is never found again' (Franklin).

Arabesque. A ballet position in which the dancer has one leg extended horizontally backwards, the torso leaning forward and both arms outstretched.

Articulation. The point at which a word or note is sounded. *See also* **diction**.

Asymmetrical. *See* **symmetry**.

Attitude. In dance, a form of **arabesque** in which one leg is held up behind the torso, with the leg bent at the knee.

Baroque. Refers to music (and art and architecture) typical of the period of about 1600–1750.

Beat. In metrical music, the underlying pulse.

Binary form. The form of a piece (normally of dance or music) that is in two sections (AB).

Blocking. In drama, the process by which a director determines the positioning of actors in the performance space and their flow within that space.

Blue note. In music, a note in a **diatonic** scale that has been flattened so that it sounds more melancholic (blue).

Blues scale. In music, a scale in which some pitches (blue notes) are performed flatter than their counterparts in a major scale. The most commonly altered pitches are the third and seventh degrees.

Body language. The non-verbal communication that performers use either consciously or subconsciously, including **posture**, **gesture** and facial expression.

Cadence. In music, a point of repose at the end of a phrase, sometimes harmonised with two cadence chords.

Call and response. A type of music in which a soloist sings or plays a phrase to which another soloist or group responds with an answering phrase.

Canon. In dance and music, a device in which one part is repeated exactly while the first part continues to unfold.

Catharsis. The release of pent-up emotions that audience members are said to feel when they see similar emotions exaggerated to breaking-point on stage.

Characterisation. In drama, the way in which the personality traits, thoughts and instincts of a character are portrayed by how the actor speaks, moves and uses physicality.

Choral speech. In drama, the declamation of words in unison by a chorus.

Chord. In music, two or more notes played at the same time with the intention of producing a harmonic effect.

Chord sequence. A series of chords. *See also* **harmonic progression**.

Choreography. In dance, the design or arrangement of steps, motifs, movements and scenes to shape and craft a piece. The completed choreography is often notated for dancers to use. *See also* **notation**.

Chromatic notes. *See* **diatonic and chromatic**.

Chromatic scale. A scale of semitones that includes all 12 pitches commonly used in western music.

Classical. Refers to: 1. Art music of any period or country as opposed to folk, jazz or popular music. 2. European art music, or music in European art-music styles, written in the second half of the 18th century and early 19th century. 3. The cultures of ancient Greece and Rome or art influenced by them. 4. Ballet in which the movement is based on the traditional techniques and in which the form or line is more important than the dramatic or emotional content.

Climax. The point of maximum intensity and possibly interest in a performance work.

Coda. In dance and music, the final section of a movement or piece.

Commedia dell'arte. A form of drama dating from northern Italy in the middle of the 16th century, involving an exaggerated style of physical acting and relying on the use of masks and **stock characters**.

Compose. To devise a piece of original music.

Consonance and dissonance. In music, the relative stability (consonance) or instability (dissonance) of two or more notes sounded simultaneously. Consonant intervals and chords are called concords. Dissonant intervals and chords are called discords.

Contact improvisation. A form of dance influenced by gymnastics which is based on giving and taking weight. Dancers need to have a high level of trust in their fellow performers in order to perform the falls, leans and lifts.

Contrast. The intentional juxtaposing of sections or passages of differing levels of volume, pacing or intensity to create a change of effect for the audience.

Corps de ballet. An ensemble of ballet dancers in a company.

Counterpoint. In music, the simultaneous combination of two or more melodic lines.

Cover version. An arrangement of a song performed by different musicians from those in the original recording.

Cross rhythm. In music, a rhythm that conflicts with the regular pattern of stressed and unstressed beats of a composition, or the combination of two conflicting rhythms within a single beat (e.g. duplets against triplets).

Denouement. In drama, the point at which the various strands of the play come together and are resolved.

Devise. To make up or assemble an original piece of performance work. In music, the word **compose** is generally used to mean the same thing.

Dialectic. A form of debate in which opposing viewpoints are reconciled in a valid conclusion.

Dialogue. In drama, a section of speech or conversation for two or more characters.

Diatonic and chromatic. In music, diatonic notes are those belonging to the scale of the prevailing key while chromatic notes are foreign to it. For example, in C major, G is a diatonic note whereas G♯ is a chromatic note.

Diction. The clarity with which a word or speech is uttered. *See also* **articulation**.

Didactic. Designed to educate an audience on a specific issue as well as, or instead of, entertaining them.

Directorial concept. The vision that the director has that determines the decisions taken to achieve the realisation of the performance.

Discrete. Separate or existing in its own right. For example, dance is a discrete art form, but is often integrated with music and drama.

Dissonance. *See* **consonance and dissonance**.

Doubling. In music, two players or groups performing the same musical line simultaneously.

Downstage. *See* **upstage and downstage**.

Dramatic irony. An effect which occurs when the audience knows something that the characters do not, and so sees a meaning or contradiction in their words of which the characters are unaware. *See also* **irony**.

Dress rehearsal. The last rehearsal before the final performance, in which the intention is for everything to be as much like the final performance as possible. Performers whose parts require costume will wear it for this rehearsal.

Dumbshow. A dramatic piece or passage in which mime is used wholly or predominantly.

Duologue. In drama, a passage for two actors. *See also* **monologue**.

Dynamics. 1. In dance, the intensity and quality of movement used, for example whether it is light or heavy, sudden or sustained. 2. In music, the relative volume.

Empathy. The ability to identify with and understand someone else's feelings or situation.

End-on stage. A style of performance space in which the stage is at one of the short ends of a rectangle, with the audience occupying the body of the rectangle and perhaps vantage points on the three facing walls.

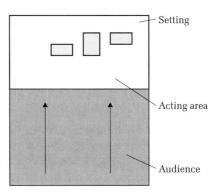

Ensemble. A group of three or more performers.

Epic theatre. A style of theatre, developed by Erwin Piscator and expanded by Bertolt Brecht in the 1920s and 1930s, that tackled large-scale, often political issues.

Epilogue. The closing section of a piece, often a monologue spoken directly to the audience. *See also* **prologue**.

Episodic. Referring to performance that is divided into episodes, which may be separate or non-linear.

Exposition. An explanation of the meaning or purpose of an issue. In drama, the part of a play that provides the audience with necessary background information, so that they understand the play's action and characters.

Exposure. The extent of a performer's prominence in the overall performance. In practical work, students must ensure that they adhere to the maximum and minimum times that are specified for the size of their group.

Fingerprint. The stylistic features that are typical of a practitioner's way of working.

Flexed. In dance, describes feet with the toes pulled up towards the leg, the opposite of pointed. Flexed feet are associated with Martha Graham's technique.

Floor work. In dance, exercises or sections of a piece in which parts of the body other than the feet are taking the body weight.

Fluency. The ability to give a smooth and uninterrupted performance of a piece.

Folk. Refers to the style of an art form such as music or dance that developed among the ordinary people of a region or culture and has been passed down from generation to generation.

Form. The style and structure of a piece.

Generic. Referring to general points common to a group, rather than specific points characteristic of an individual.

Genre. The category to which a piece belongs, defined by elements such as its style, form and content.

Gesture. The use of expressive movements or expressions to create meaning in performance.

Gestus or **Gest**. In the drama developed by Brecht, the use of stylised movement and physicality to represent the essential features of a character and their relationships to other characters.

Harmonic progression. In music, a series of chords.

Harmonic rhythm. In music, a rhythmic pattern made by chord changes. Harmonic rhythm is often different from the rhythm of the melody.

Harmonic sequence. In music, the immediate repetition of a progression of chords at a higher or lower pitch level.

Harmony. In music, the combination of sounds to produce a chord or a progression of chords.

Heel-to-toe. A dance move in which the floor is touched by the heel and then the toe. When the toe is in contact with the floor, the heel may not be lifted.

Hot-seating. In drama, the method of a group questioning an actor in role to investigate how the character would react to different questions.

Improvisation. The spontaneous creation of a performance work through performing.

Influences. Pre-existing styles and individual works that have a determining effect on the work of a specific practitioner.

Integration. In this course, the bringing together of art forms, as opposed to allowing them to operate in isolation from one another.

Internalise. To make something personal to oneself and one's beliefs.

In the round. A performance setting in which the audience surrounds the performers, with the performance taking place in the central space:

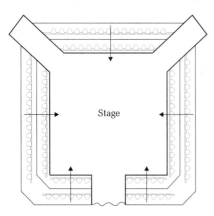

Irony. In drama, the effect created by the humorous or satirical use of language in order to make the opposite comment from what is seemingly being said. *See also* **dramatic irony**.

Jazz 1. A form of music characterised by vocal and instrumental improvisation, an insistent march-like beat, complex syncopation, blue notes and simple formulaic harmonic progressions. 2. In dance, a style influenced by jazz music, with dancing off the beat and staccato movement that lacks the flow of ballet.

Jeté. In ballet, a leap in which the dancer jumps off one foot and lands on the other.

Juxtaposition. The placing of different things side by side to create a desired effect.

Key. In music, the relationship between the pitches of notes in which one particular pitch is more important than other pitches. This note is called the tonic and its pitch determines the key of the music. So a composition in which C is the tonic is said to be 'in the key of C'.

Key signature. In music, one or more flat (♭) or sharp (♯) signs placed immediately after a clef (𝄞, 𝄢) or double bar line on a stave. The effect of each flat or sharp sign lasts throughout the stave and applies to all notes with the same letter name unless contradicted by accidentals or a change in key signature. A key signature usually gives some indication of the key of the music that follows it.

Language. 1. The elements of communication. The language of performing arts is the way in which the elements of performance in dance, drama and music work together to communicate to an audience. 2. In drama, the words used by a character that convey a particular location, period, social class and so on.

Legato. In music, a smooth performance without any breaks between successive notes. *See also* **staccato**.

Levels. 1. In dance and drama, blocks and scaffolding can be used to vary the levels of the performers in order to vary the arrangement that the audience sees. 2. In dance, there are three basic levels of movement: low (on the floor), mid (standing level) and high (jumping, being lifted or thrown).

Linear narrative. *See* **narrative**.

Lyrics. The text of a song.

Major and minor. In music, a major interval is greater than a minor interval by a semitone. The interval between the first and third degrees of a major scale is four semitones, one semitone greater than the interval between the same degrees in a minor scale.

Medley. An arrangement in which two or more songs are linked to produce a continuous performance. Medleys of songs are often by the same songwriter or from the same show, or from the same style and period.

Melody. The line of a piece of music (often a song) where choice and arrangement of pitch, duration and intervals are intended to provide primary interest. *See also* **accompaniment**.

Metaphor. A literary device in which one thing is described through a comparison to something else, but without the use of a word such as 'like' or 'as'. For example, 'All the world's a stage'. *See also* **simile**.

Metronome mark. A note value plus an equals sign and a number, given at the beginning of a composition. The note value is the beat and the number shows how many beats there should be per minute. Thus ♩ = 60 means there should be 60 crotchet beats per minute.

Minimalism. In music, a style developed in the 1960s that reduced the elements of music to the bare essentials.

Minor. *See* **major and minor**.

Mise-en-scène. In drama, the arrangement of everything put on the stage, such as scenery, props, lighting, costume and actors, to represent the setting of that particular moment in the play.

Modulation. The harmonic or melodic process by which a piece of music moves from one key to another.

Monologue. In drama, a speech of some significance given by a single actor. *See also* **duologue**, **soliloquy**.

Monotimbral. Refers to music written for an instrument of only one timbre. If the part is doubled, this is done by the same timbre (e.g. two violins playing the same melody).

Mood. The emotional effect created by a practitioner and by performers. This can be through visual elements such as set and lighting (bright, dark, dull, colourful and so on), through sound effects, through elements of music such as style, tempo and key, through language and tone.

Motif. A short idea or fragment that may form the basis of a longer piece of work. It is sufficiently distinctive to allow it to be modified, manipulated and possibly combined with other motifs while retaining its own identity.

Multi-role playing. In drama, a style in which one actor plays more than one role.

Muscle memory. Memory of movements that have been repeatedly practised and are consequently performed by the body without the performer having to think about carrying them out.

Music hall. Variety entertainment that was popular between about 1880 and 1930, usually a sequence of song, dance, circus shows, comedy and other acts by different performers.

Narrative. A performance that tells a story. Linear narrative tells a story in chronological order, beginning by setting the scene and introducing the characters, then relating the events leading to the climax of the action and its resolution. Non-linear narrative also tells a story, but jumps around, making use of devices such as flashbacks, and expects the audience to work out a lot of the implicit details for themselves.

Narrator. In drama, a character, inside or outside of the action, who tells or comments on the story.

Neutral. Refers to a dance position in which the feet are placed parallel to each other and slightly apart, the body and neck are relaxed, and the arms are straight but relaxed by the sides of the body.

Notation. 1. In music, staff notation consists of a stave, a clef and notes printed on, between, above or below the lines of the stave. Music can also be written out in a graphic score using symbols. 2. In dance, two systems of notation are currently in use: Laban and Benesh. Labanotation uses shapes and symbols to indicate the body part involved in the movement, and the direction, level and length of time of the movement. Benesh notation uses symbols to plot the movements of the body along a five-line stave. Choreographers also use stick men or computer programs such as LifeForms.

Orchestrate. To arrange a piece of music for orchestral performance.

Ostinato. In music, a rhythmic, melodic or harmonic pattern played many times in succession.

Pace. The speed at which the action, events or music moves along.

Palindrome. A piece of work that is the same backwards as forwards. At the mid-point, the work starts to mirror the first half. The words 'noon' 'level' and 'madam' are examples of palindromes.

Parable. A story that demonstrates a moral lesson.

Parody. A deliberately amusing imitation.

Pathway. In dance, the route traced by the body or a body part as it performs a movement or motif.

Pedestrian movement. In dance, movement based on everyday movements such as walking, tripping over or reaching for a glass.

Pentatonic. Refers to music based on a scale of five different pitches.

Performance space. The three-dimensional area in which a performer works. *See also* **end-on stage**, **in the round**, **thrust stage** and **traverse stage**.

Phasing. In music, a compositional device in which two identical short lines start together and repeat over and over again, gradually moving out of synchronisation and then coming back together.

Phrase. 1. In music, part of a melody that requires the addition of another phrase or phrases to make complete musical sense. 2. In dance, a section of movement.

Physicality. The bodily, as opposed to facial or verbal, aspects of performance.

Physical theatre. A style of performance that places physical expression and movement at the centre of the performance. The style embraces elements of dance and drama and is associated with the work of Steven Berkoff and Lloyd Newson and DV8.

Pitch. In music, the height or depth of a note. This can be expressed in relatively vague terms ('the pitch of that note is A', or even 'that is a high-pitched note'), or it can be expressed in absolute terms ('the pitch of this A is 440 vibrations per second').

Plié. A ballet movement in which the knees are bent and the feet are turned out. In a deep plié, the heels are raised from the ground. In a demi-plié, which is not as deep, the heels remain on the ground.

Posture. The way in which a performer holds their body when performing.

Prima ballerina. The main female dancer in a ballet company.

Prologue. In drama, the opening section of a work, sometimes involving a spoken monologue. *See also* **epilogue**.

Properties. Items of furniture, equipment or costume necessary for performers to use on stage. Often abbreviated to 'props'.

Proscenium arch. A form of theatre design in which the audience is separated from the performers, the performance taking place on a (normally raised) stage framed by an arch.

Prose. Text that is not put together using any kind of metrical or rhyming structure. *See also* **verse**.

Proxemics. The placing of performers in a piece and the spatial relationship between each of them and between the performers and the audience.

Pulse. Beat.

Range. In music, the distance between the lowest and highest notes of a melody or composition, or the distance between the highest and lowest notes that can be played on an instrument or sung by a particular type of voice.

Realisation. The re-creation of a performance work from notation, recording or script.

Realism. A style in which things are made to look and sound as they do in real life, rather than looking deliberately staged.

Recitative. In music, a solo song in free rhythms that mirror the rhythms of the text. The pitches of a recitative also mirror the rise and fall of the speaking voice and often express the emotional significance of the text.

Reflective practitioner. A practitioner who is able to learn by reflecting on the effectiveness of what they have produced so far.

Refrain. In music, a repeated passage, such as the chorus of a pop song.

Rehearse. To practise a piece until it is at a standard where all of the performers are completely in control of their roles demonstrating total performance memory.

Relationships. In dance, the way in which performers work on their own or together in various combinations such as solo, duet, trio and so on.

Repertoire. Pieces of performance work created by established practitioners.

Reprise. The repetition of a previous phrase or theme.

Rhythm. In music, the pattern with which a composer organises the relative lengths and stresses of notes.

Rhythmic augmentation. In music, the lengthening of time values of the notes of a melody.

Rondo form. In dance and music, a form in which the opening section is repeated several times, the repeats being separated from each other by contrasting passages known as episodes.

Rubato. Flexibility in the tempo of music, with some notes played for longer than their written value and others for less time.

Run-through. An unpolished performance of a piece undertaken in the performance process to help performers gain an understanding of the structure of the piece as a whole.

Scale. In music, a collection of pitches played or sung in stepwise ascending or descending order.

Scene. In drama, a short section, often separated by a scene change in which the arrangement of the stage may be changed.

Score. In music, a printed or written copy of all of the parts in a composition, laid out underneath one another.

Seamless. Refers to performance work in which the transitions are woven into the piece so as not to stand out.

Serial music. Music based on manipulating a fixed series of 12 notes, including every pitch of a chromatic scale.

Simile. A literary device in which one thing is compared to another in order to draw attention to specific features of it. For example, 'Her eyes shone like the stars'. *See also* **metaphor**.

Soft-shoe. A style of tap in which the shoes have soft soles, ensuring a softer sound when the foot makes contact with the floor.

Soliloquy. A monologue that is delivered directly to the audience.

Song plugger. A pianist/singer who worked in Tin Pan Alley, New York in the early part of the 20th century, selling the sheet music for popular songs.

Soundscape. A collage of sound effects and music, put together to create a kind of aural backdrop to a scene.

Space. *See* **performance space**.

Sprung. In dance, refers to a specialised floor that has built-in spring in order to make it safe for jumping on.

Staccato. In music, refers to notes that are separated from others in a phrase, often with a slight extra attack. *See also* **legato**.

Stanza. A verse of a song or poem.

Stasis. In dance, stillness; the opposite of movement.

Status. The level of power of a particular character or role.

Stereotype. In drama, a character built out of personality traits assumed to be typical of a social class, ethnic group or other recognisable stock character, not individualised.

Strophic song. A song in which the same music is used for every stanza (verse) of the text, though the words for the verses differ.

Structure. The way in which a piece of dance, drama or music is put together – the sections it comprises and how these are arranged in relation to one another.

Style. The way in which a practitioner organises their performance materials or the manner in which the piece is performed, often building on the work of other practitioners.

Subtext. In drama, the realities of a situation that are not made explicit in the dialogue but that are communicated to the audience through facial expressions, actions or asides.

Symmetry. A symmetrical image reflects itself. If you imagine a line drawn down the centre of the image, you should see that the two halves are mirror images of one another. In the opposite, an **asymmetrical** image, the two sides do not mirror one another.

Syncopation. In music, accentuation of notes sounded off the beat or on a weak beat.

Tableau. A group of performers who freeze in a particular way to create an image for the audience.

Tango. A Latin American dance in syncopated $\frac{4}{4}$ time or the music to accompany such a dance.

Tempo. The speed of a performance, usually measured by speed of the beat. This can be indicated by a metronome mark (e.g. ♩ = 120), a written instruction (e.g moderato), or both.

Tension. The feeling of anxious suspense created by points of climax or conflict within a piece that engage and sustain the audience's interest.

Ternary form. A three-part structure (ABA) in which the first and last sections are identical or very similar. These enclose a contrasting central section.

Texture. In music, the number and timbre of parts in a composition and the way in which they relate to each other.

Theme. 1. The subject of a piece, or a more abstract idea that runs through a play or dance. 2. A melodic unit that recurs several times in a piece of music, sometimes altered but consistently recognisable. In both 1 and 2, the theme is a structural element, providing a link between the various parts.

Thrust stage. A performance space that brings the actors out into the audience, who sit on three sides of the stage.

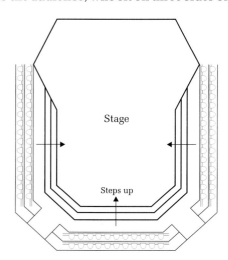

Timbre. In music, the tone and colour of an instrument or voice.

Timing. The ability of performers to deliver a particular contribution to a piece at the best moment for it to create maximum impact in the performance situation.

Tonal. Refers to music based in an identifiable key.

Torso. The trunk of the human body.

Transcribe. To write musical notation from listening to a recorded performance.

Transition. The means by which a piece moves from one episode, scene or section to another.

Transpose. In music, to perform or notate a passage or whole piece at a pitch-level higher or lower than the original.

Travelling. In dance, movement used to transfer the dancer from one spot to another, for example skipping, running, hopping, rolling, dragging and jumping.

Traverse stage. A stage which runs between two auditorium areas, enabling the action to sweep along it.

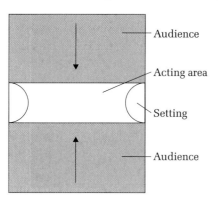

Triad. In music, a chord of three pitches consisting of a fundamental pitch called the root and notes pitched a 3rd and a 5th above it.

Turning. In dance, circular movement of the body performed on one or two feet. Turns can be performed on the spot, while travelling across the stage, or in the air as part of a jump. A quarter turn means that the body turns through 90 degrees, a half turn through 180 degrees and a full turn through the full 360 degrees of a circle.

Unison. 1. In music, the combined sound of two or more notes of the same pitch. 2. In dance and drama, the simultaneous performance of movements or the simultaneous speaking of the same lines.

Upstage and downstage. The back and front of the stage, respectively. The terminology stems from theatres of the 18th century in which the back of the stage was elevated slightly so that the audience had a clearer view.

Upstaging. Placing one character behind, or upstage, of another. Most of the time it involves the character downstage in some form of critical, satirical unspoken comment on the one upstaged.

Vaudeville. American equivalent of **music hall**.

Verfremdungseffekt. A technique developed by Bertolt Brecht. The distancing or 'making strange' of an event or character through the stripping away of familiar qualities and creating a new sense of astonishment or curiosity about them.

Verse. Poetry written using a metrical structure, with the words are arranged to produce, for example, a specific number of syllables in a line or a particular rhythm.

Volume. In music, the dynamic measure of sound in a performance.

Word painting. In music, the representation of the meaning of words in the rhythm or pitch of a melody (e.g. the word 'high' might be set to a high note).